EAST USSEX COUN

PLAYS
THE BOY WITH A CART
THE FIRSTBORN
VENUS OBSERVED

D1188849

CHRISTOPHER FRY

PLAYS

The Boy with a Cart

The Firstborn

Venus Observed

OXFORD UNIVERSITY PRESS

LONDON OXFORD NEW YORK

1970

Oxford University Press

LONDON OXFORD NEW YORK

GLASGOW TORONTO MELBOURNE WELLINGTON

CAPE TOWN SALISBURY IBADAN NAIROBI LUSAKA DAR ES SALAAM ADDIS ABABA

BOMBAY CALCUTTA MADRAS KARACHI LAHORE DACCA

KUALA LUMPUR SINGAPORE HONG KONG TOKYO

© Christopher Fry 1949, 1952, 1958

The Boy with a Cart first published by Oxford University Press, London, 1939. Second edition published by Frederick Muller Ltd., 1945, and reprinted in this Oxford Paperbacks edition by permission of the publishers

The Firstborn first published by the Cambridge University Press, 1946. Reissued by Oxford University Press, London, 1949; second edition (revised) 1952; third edition 1958

Venus Observed first published by Oxford University Press, London, 1950

The three plays first published as an Oxford University Press paperback 1970

No performance or reading of these plays may be given unless a licence has been obtained in advance from the author's agents, ACTAC Ltd., 16 CADOGAN LANE, LONDON, S.W.1, and no copy of the plays or any part thereof may be reproduced for any purpose whatsoever by any printing or duplicating or photographic or other method without written permission obtained in advance from the publishers. Non-observance of the above stipulations constitutes a breach of copyright.

For special stipulations regarding amateur performances of *The Boy with a Cart* see p. 2.

EAST SUSSEX

V. MAC 3012

CLASS No. 822.912

BOOK No. 587062 731

COUNTY LIBRARY

PRINTED IN GREAT BRITAIN

1928108847

CONTENTS

THE BOY WITH A CART

CUTHMAN, SAINT OF SUSSEX

A Play

SECOND EDITION

All rights reserved. An acting fee is payable on each and every performance of this play. For information regarding the fee for amateur performances application should be made to: J. GARNET MILLER LTD., *1/5 Portpool Lane, London, E.C. 1, or to the following agents:*

Great Britain: Theatricals, 91 Snow Hill, Birmingham 4.
Philip Son & Nephew Ltd., 7 Whitechapel, Liverpool 1.
R. Sheldon Bamber Ltd., 12 & 13 Charing Cross Mansions, Glasgow, C. 3.

Eire: Fred Hanna Ltd., 28 & 29 Nassau Street, Dublin, C. 3.

Australia: Will Andrade, 173 Pitt Street (G.P.O. Box 3111), Sydney.

New Zealand: Pat Bell McKenzie, The Play Bureau, 7 Disraeli Street, Hawera.

South Africa: Darters Ltd., P.O. Box 174, Cape Town.

U.S.A.:   Walter H. Baker Company, 100 Summer Street, Boston, Mass.

To

BARRY MANN

the first CUTHMAN

THE BOY WITH A CART

First performed at Coleman's Hatch, Sussex,
1938
Revived at the Lyric Theatre, Hammersmith,
16 January 1950

Cuthman . .	RICHARD BURTON
Bess	HAZEL TERRY
Mildred ⎫ Mrs. Fipps ⎭ . . .	DIANA GRAVES
Matt	LEE FOX
Tibb	JOHN KIDD
Cuthman's mother . .	MARY JERROLD
Tawm	NOËL WILLMAN
His daughter . .	HARRIETTE JOHNS
His son-in-law . .	ADRIAN CAIRNS
A farmer . . .	OLAF POOLEY
Alfred	DAVID OXLEY
Demiwulf . .	ROBERT MARSDEN

Directed by John Gielgud

CHARACTERS

(In order of appearance)

CUTHMAN

BESS AND MILDRED

MATT AND TIBB   } *Cornish neighbours*

CUTHMAN'S MOTHER

TAWM

HIS DAUGHTER

HIS SON-IN-LAW

A FARMER   } *Villagers of Steyning*

ALFRED AND

DEMIWULF, THE SONS OF

MRS. FIPPS

*Cornish neighbours, mowers, villagers of Steyning,
and The People of South England*

Extracts from two songs by Richard Addinsell (*from the composer's manuscript*)

THE PEOPLE OF SOUTH ENGLAND.

In our fields, fallow and burdened, in grass and furrow,
In barn and stable, with scythe, flail, or harrow,
Sheepshearing, milking or mowing, on labour that's older
Than knowledge, with God we work shoulder to shoulder;
God providing, we dividing, sowing, and pruning;
Not knowing yet and yet sometimes discerning:
Discerning a little at Spring when the bud and shoot
With pointing finger show the hand at the root,
With stretching finger point the mood in the sky:
Sky and root in joint action; and the cry
Of the unsteady lamb allying with the brief
Sunlight, with the curled and cautious leaf.

Coming out from our doorways on April evenings
When tomorrow's sky is written on the slates
We have discerned a little, we have learned
More than the gossip that comes to us over our gates.
We have seen old men cracking their memories for dry milk.
We have seen old women dandling shadows;
But coming out from our doorways, we have felt
Heaven ride with Spring into the meadows.

We have felt the joint action of root and sky, of man
And God, when day first risks the hills, and when
The darkness hangs the hatchet in the barn
And scrapes the heavy boot against the iron:
In first and last twilight, before wheels have turned
Or after they are still, we have discerned:
Guessed at divinity working above the wind,
Working under our feet; or at the end
Of a furrow, watching the lark dissolve in sun,
We have almost known, a little have known

The work that is with our work, as we have seen
The blackthorn hang where the Milky Way has been:
Flower and star spattering the sky
And the root touched by some divinity.

   Coming out from our doorways on October nights
   We have seen the sky unfreeze and a star drip
   Into the south: experienced alteration
   Beyond experience. We have felt the grip
   Of the hand on earth and sky in careful coupling
   Despite the jibbing, man destroying, denying,
   Disputing, or the late frost looting the land
   Of green. Despite flood and the lightning's rifle
   In root and sky we can discern the hand.

It is there in the story of Cuthman, the working together
Of man and God like root and sky; the son
Of a Cornish shepherd, Cuthman, the boy with a cart,
The boy we saw trudging the sheep-tracks with his mother
Mile upon mile over five counties; one
Fixed purpose biting his heels and lifting his heart.
We saw him; we saw him with a grass in his mouth, chewing
And travelling. We saw him building at last
A church among whortleberries. And you shall see
Now, in this place, the story of his going
And his building.—A thousand years in the past
There was a shepherd, and his son had three
Sorrows come together on him. Shadow
The boy. Follow him now as he runs in the meadow.

            Enter CUTHMAN, *running. He stops short as he sees*
                     two NEIGHBOURS *approaching.*

CUTHMAN. Now, my legs, look what a bad place
   You've brought me into: Bess and Mildred coming:
   Two nice neighbours with long noses. Now
   I should like the sun to go down, and I could close
   As the daisy closes: put up my shutters, slap,

Here in the long grass. Whip the world away
In one collapsing gesture. And you can't
Waken a sleeping daisy with a shaking.—
Well, green is green and flesh is a different matter.
Green is under their feet, but my lot's better.
I can say to them Neighbours, believe it or not,
God is looking after my father's sheep.
But the simple truth is harder to tell than a lie.
The trouble I'll have, and the trouble they'll have to believe it!
And I wasn't looking for trouble this bright morning.

[*As the* NEIGHBOURS *come up to him.*

Good morning, good morning!

BESS. Good morning, Cuthman.

CUTHMAN. This is the morning to take the air, flute-clear
And, like a lutanist, with a hand of wind
Playing the responsive hills, till a long vibration
Spills across the fields, and the chancelled larches
Sing like Lenten choirboys, a green treble;
Playing at last the skylark into rising,
The wintered cuckoo to a bashful stutter.
It is the first day of the year that I've king'd
Myself on the rock, sat myself in the wind:
It was laying my face on gold. And when I stood
I felt the webs of winter all blow by
And in the bone-dry runnel of the earth
Spring restart her flood.

MILDRED.   We came to find you,
Cuthman, expecting to find you with the sheep.

CUTHMAN. Dinner-time is passed, and my father
Has forgotten where his son chews on a grass
And thinks of meat.

BESS.   Cuthman-chick, your father——

CUTHMAN. I know what you will say to me: My father
  Has my promise to be shepherd till he send
  Another boy to take my place and tend them.
  And, promise-bound, what do I do careering
  Like a stone down a hill, like a holidaymaker
  With only his own will? But they're safe,
  Those little sheep, more than with me beside them,
  More than with twenty Cuthmans now God minds them.

BESS. Cuthman-boy—

CUTHMAN.   It is so! Not today
  Only, but other days God took the crook
  And watched them in the wind. One other day
  My father let the time go by, forgetting
  To send away the herdboy to relieve me.
  However often I stood up on the rock
  Shouting 'Here's Cuthman! Here's a hungry shepherd!'
  My only relief came from the clouds that closed
  With the sun and dodged again: the sun that tacked
  From dinner-time into the afternoon.
  I was as empty as a vacant barn.
  It might have been because my stomach was empty
  That I was suddenly filled with faith—
  Suddenly parcelled with faith like a little wain
  In a good hay-season and, all round, the hills
  Lay at my feet like collies. So I took
  My crook, and round the sheep I drew a circle
  Saying 'God guard them here, if God will guard them';
  Drew it, though as a fence I knew it was less
  Good than a bubble. Then to yearling and ewe
  And lamb I said 'Give no trouble'; laid
  My crook against the rock and went to dinner.
  When I came back no lamb or yearling or ewe
  Had broken through. They gently lay together
  Cropping the crook's limited pasture, though

The unhedged green said 'Trespass.'—This is true.
Come, and I'll show you. I have waited again
To go to dinner and father has forgotten——
BESS. Cuthman, your father is dead.
MILDRED.   We came to tell you.
CUTHMAN. You can't say that to me. I was speaking the truth.
MILDRED. We were speaking the truth.
CUTHMAN.   You came to make me sorry,
But you're breaking the sun over your knees to say
My father's dead. My father is strong and well.
Each morning my father buckles himself to,
Like a leather strap, and at night comes to the fire
His hands bare with well-water to tell
The story of Jesus. So he will talk tonight,
Clenching his hands against Gethsemane,
Opening his hands to feel the Ascension
As though after dry weeks he were feeling
The first rain. Every evening I have watched,
And his face was like a live coal under the smoking
Shadows on the ceiling.
BESS.   What can we do,
Cuthman, if you're unbelieving?
MILDRED.   Come
Down with us and see him.
CUTHMAN.   Let me alone.
No; if I come you'll take me to a place
Where truth will laugh and scatter like a magpie.
Up here, my father waits for me at home
And God sits with the sheep.
BESS.   Cuthman, you make it
Hard for us to tell you.
MILDRED.   The trouble we have
To tell him, and the trouble he has to believe.

BESS. How can we help you, Cuthman, in your trouble
If our words go by like water in a sieve?

CUTHMAN. Let me alone.

MILDRED.   It's funny the way it takes him.
I don't even know if he really understands.
I don't even know if he really thinks we're lying.

BESS. Well, I don't know. Perhaps he feels like crying
And that's why he wants us to go.

MILDRED.   It may be so.

BESS [*to* CUTHMAN]. If we can be any help——

MILDRED. If there's anything we can do——

BESS. We'd better go to his mother again, poor soul,
And get her a bite or two. She's certain not
To eat a thing unless somebody's by.

MILDRED. It's a merciful thing she had the sense to cry.

[*They go away down the hill.*

CUTHMAN. What have I done? Did I steal God away
From my father to guard my sheep? How can I keep
Pace with a pain that comes in my head so fast?
How did I make the day brittle to break?
What sin brought in the strain, the ominous knock,
The gaping seam? Was it a boast on the rock,
The garrulous game? What have I done to him?
Father, if you are standing by to help me—
Help me to cry.

[*He falls on the ground.*

THE PEOPLE OF SOUTH ENGLAND.
The day is pulled up by the root and dries,
And the sun drains to the hollow sea.
Heaven is quarried with cries.
Song dies on the tree.

The thongs of the daylight are drawn and slack.
The dew crawls down to earth like tears.
Root and sky break
And will not mend with prayers.

Only the minutes fall and stack
Like a rising drum
Where, thin as a draught through the crack,
Death has whistled home.

CUTHMAN [*rising to his knees*]. I have ears stopped with earth
Not to have heard the door-catch as he went,
The raven guling dew, the crow on the stack,
Nor grasped the warning of the howling dog
To bring me to my feet, to have me home;
Heard soon enough to run and still to find him;
For me to say 'You have been a father
Not to lie down so soon, not to forget
Till I forget the last hand that shall hold me.'
Still to be able to find him, and to see
How he put down his cup and dried his mouth
And turned as heaven shut behind him.

THE PEOPLE OF SOUTH ENGLAND.
How is your faith now, Cuthman?
Your faith that the warm world hatched,
That spread its unaccustomed colour
Up on the rock, game and detached?

You see how sorrow rises, Cuthman,
How sorrow rises like the heat
Even up to the plumed hills
And the quickest feet.

Pain is low against the ground
And grows like a weed.
Is God still in the air
And in the seed?

Is God still in the air
Now that the sun is down?
They are afraid in the city,
Sleepless in the town.

Cold on the roads,
Desperate by the river.
Can faith for long elude
Prevailing fever?

CUTHMAN. I have stayed too long with the children, a boy
   sliding
On the easy ice, skating the foolish silver
Over the entangling weed and the eddying water.
If I have only ventured the reflection
And not the substance, and accepted only
A brushwork sun skidding ahead of me
And not the dealer of days and docker of time;
Only the blue-print of a star and not
The star; accepted only the light's boundary
To the shadow and not the shadow, only the gloss
And burnish of the leaf and not the leaf—
Let me see now with truer sight, O God
Of root and sky; let me at last be faithful
In perception, and in action that is born
Of perception, even as I have been faithful
In the green recklessness of little knowledge.
Grant this, O God, that I may grow to my father
As he grew to Thy Son, and be his son
Now and for always.

VOICES OF NEIGHBOURS. Cuthman! Cuthman! Cuthman!

CUTHMAN. Here's the valley breaking against the hill.

PEOPLE OF ENGLAND. Sorrow rises like the heat.

CUTHMAN. No longer dryshod can I keep my will.

PEOPLE OF ENGLAND. Nor the plumed feet.

CUTHMAN. The circle is broken and the sheep wander.
   They pull the branches of the myrtle under:
   Nibble the shadow of the cypress, trample
   The yew, and break the willow of its tears.
   This is no grief of theirs.

                    [*Two* NEIGHBOURS, MATT *and* TIB, *come up to him.*

MATT.   Cuthman, your father
   Is dead.

CUTHMAN. They told me.

TIB.   Your mother is sick.

CUTHMAN.   She is grieving.

MATT. She is calling for you. We heard her voice through the
   window.

CUTHMAN. I shall come soon. But the sheep are foot-loose and
   green-
   Hungry. They will be lost in sundown, and no
   Bell-wether. Where would my mother tell me to go,
   To her or bring them home?

TIB.   You have no home,
   Cuthman.

CUTHMAN. I have no father, but my mother
   Is at home.

MATT.   Your home is sold over your head.
   There's no roof over your sorrow: nor a patch
   Of ground to know your name in; nothing, son,
   Nothing in the valley.

CUTHMAN.   My mother's at home.

TIB. Your mother is sick. What will you do, Cuthman?

CUTHMAN. I will drive my father's sheep home to my mother.

                              [*Exit* CUTHMAN.

MATT. Could we have told him the rest of it: the last
   Of the rotten business?

TIB.   I had said enough.
I had done more damage with words than downpour
Did the crops. Look how his wing is dragging.

MATT. Look what he still has to know. His Father dead,
The house sold over his head, and still the blow,
The final straw: no money in the house,
Not a flip of silver he can toss,
And double in his hand.

TIB.   But still we said
Enough. And what we said he scarcely knows.
He carries the first trouble, and the rest
Only dog at his heels.

MATT.   Make your way down.
None of us knows the way a neighbour feels.

                                        [*Exeunt.*

THE PEOPLE OF SOUTH ENGLAND.
    Out of this, out of the first incision
    Of mortality on mortality, there comes
    The genuflexion, and the partition of pain
    Between man and God; there grows the mutual action,
    The perspective to the vision.
    Out of this, out of the dereliction
    Of a mild morning, comes the morning's motive,
    The first conception, the fusion of root and sky;
    Grows the achievement of the falling shadow,
    Pain's patient benediction.

NEIGHBOURS [*entering*].
    One after the other we have gone to the boy,
    Offering him advice, condolences, and recommendations
    To relations in more well-to-do places.
    We have offered him two good meals a day.—
    My wife is a bad cook but she gives large helpings.—
    We have done what we could; we can't do more.

But he goes his own way. All that we say
He seems to ignore. He keeps himself apart,
Speaking only out of politeness,
Eating out his heart, and of all things on earth
He is making a cart!

One after the other we have gone to him and said,
'Cuthman, what use will a cart be to you?'
He scarcely so much as raised his head, only
Shook it, saying, 'I will tell you some other time;
I am in a hurry.'

One after the other we have gone also
To his mother, offering advice, condolences,
Recommendations to our distant relations.
His poor mother, she suffers a great deal in her legs.
And we have said to her, 'We hope you will excuse
Our asking, we hope you will not think us
Inquisitive, but what is your boy Cuthman
So busy on?'—And she replied each time:
'It is something after his own heart.'

We are none the wiser: and after all
It is none of our business, though it's only natural
We should take a certain amount of interest.

One after the other we have gone indoors
Turning it over in our minds as we went
About our chores. What will the old woman do,
Dear heart, with no roof over her head, no man,
No money, and her boy doing nothing
But make a cart?

'I will tell you some other time,' he said.
'I am in a hurry.' Well, that's his look-out.
It's not for us to worry.

[*They go back to the village.*

Enter CUTHMAN *with a cart, and his* MOTHER.

CUTHMAN. If you turn round, Mother, you can see the village almost under your feet. You won't get another view. It's sinking like a ship. We're looking at the last of it.

MOTHER. My legs, my legs! That hill's finished them. I should have stopped at the bottom. Your grandmother used to say to me when I was a girl: 'Daughter,' she would say, 'never get above yourself. It will be your downfall.' Little did she guess what things would happen to me, and it's just as well, I was her favourite daughter.

CUTHMAN. We shall never see it again; we shall never look again at the sun on the white walls, my swaddling-clothes put out to dry. I am out of them once and for all.

MOTHER. What on earth are you doing talking about your swaddling clothes? I wish I knew what was the matter with you. You were shortened at five months. You were walking at a year. . . . Dear heart, I don't know how ever I got up as far as I have.

CUTHMAN. I have never known anything except the village and these few hills. I have two eyes, but how can I know if I have a memory for faces? I have two legs, but they've only carried me backwards and forwards like an old flight of steps. All my life I have been on a tether, but now I have slipped it and the world is green from side to side.

MOTHER. You know nothing of the world, Cuthman, and I'm thankful to say it. I am an old woman and I know too much. I have seen it. I've seen too much of it. Before I married your father I worked as a laundress at Letherwithel. That's fourteen miles away. And after we were married he brought me here, fourteen miles sitting behind him on a horse.

CUTHMAN. But now you're going to travel in style; we've got a cart for you to ride in.

MOTHER [*looking at the cart and back at* CUTHMAN]. Sometimes I think you can't be very well, Cuthman. . . . Your father and I first met one October. He had ridden over to the fair and it came on to rain.

CUTHMAN. We have more than fourteen miles to go. Last night I looked up and saw the full moon standing behind a tree. It was like a strange man walking into the room at night without knocking. It made my heart jump. . . . I don't know how many miles we'll have to go.

MOTHER. Cuthman! Look your mother in the face. What are you going to do with her?

CUTHMAN. We're going to travel.

MOTHER. I wish I knew what to do with you. The trouble is, you don't give me time to speak. You rush me up a hill so that I lose all my breath. You won't listen to reason. Where are you taking me? I insist upon knowing—don't think you can get away with those mysterious wags of your head. I shan't take another step until I know.

CUTHMAN. We're going to see the world, Mother.

MOTHER. I'm an old woman and I won't be joked to. Who gave you this man's address?

CUTHMAN. I haven't got an address, Mother.

MOTHER. I'm going to be very ill.   [*She sits on the cart.*

CUTHMAN. We shall find our way in the world, Mother, and I've made you a cart. You can rest as you go.

MOTHER. I've always stood up for you to the neighbours. They have come to me often enough and said: 'Cuthman isn't practical; he's going to find life very difficult.' And I have always said to them: 'Never you mind. Cuthman's my son, and when I was a girl his grandmother used to say to me, "Daughter, whatever else you may be, you have your wits."'—And in the end, after all the trouble I've had to bring you up, you want to use me like a barrowful of turnips.

CUTHMAN. Mother, can you remember the neighbours' faces when you came into the village riding on the back of my father's horse?

MOTHER. The neighbours' faces? I should think so indeed, like yesterday. They were all stuck out of the windows and they were shouting out to each other, 'What do you think of that? He's gone out of his way to find something!' They liked the look of me at once, they told me afterwards. We have always been very respected in the village.

CUTHMAN. That's just it; so it wouldn't do at all to end your days as a beggar in the place where you've always been respected; it wouldn't do to end them in a little hovel that some one would let us have, in a corner of one of their sheds, living on their left-overs and perhaps a good meal at Christmas.

MOTHER. This is the finish of me, I can't survive it. There wasn't a day in the week that I didn't have a clean apron. And now there's no one to look after me except a fool of a son, and he wants to trundle me all over the world like a load of fish.

CUTHMAN. What do you think I have been doing, Mother, while I sat all day on the doorstep, working at the cart? You couldn't get a whistle or a word out of me. But I've been thinking and praying; and wherever we go, if we go wisely and faithfully, God will look after us. Calamity is the forking of the roads, and when we have gone a little way up the turn we shall find it equally green. We have nibbled the old pasture bare, and now we must look for longer grass.

MOTHER. I'm too old for it, too old for it. The world's no greener than a crab in the sea, and I don't like its nip. . . . Oh, what a disaster! What a wealth of affliction! Nothing between me and the weather except my second-best bombasine!

CUTHMAN. You'll see; after a bit, and after a bit of worry per-haps, we shall come into our own again. You'll find yourself say-ing, 'This is just the place for us; just what we wanted.' And there'll be work for me to do. I shall buckle myself to every morning, and you shall have a white apron. These last days, while I sat on the step, I prayed. I was praying while I worked at the cart.

MOTHER. That's the best thing; it's always the best thing. I have been praying too. But I'm an old woman and I know the dangers. The world's a bothering place, that's what I can't make you see: the world isn't Heaven and I know it well.

CUTHMAN. But the world has more than one hill and valley and that's the comfort of it. Get easy, Mother; we're leaving.

MOTHER. I'm sick at the thought of it. Your grandmother would cry herself into her grave if she were alive to see us.

CUTHMAN. But as it is nobody is crying.

[*He turns and looks for the last time at the village.*

MOTHER [*as they go*]. It is just as well that we went away respected; that will be something to remember at any rate. I told the villagers, 'We are going away; Cuthman has found work to do.'

CUTHMAN. And hard work, too, Mother, if there are many hills. You're no feather.

[*They set off on their journey, the* MOTHER *in the cart, and a rope round* CUTHMAN'S *neck attached to the handles. As they go* CUTHMAN *begins to whistle. They are heard going away into the distance.*

THE PEOPLE OF SOUTH ENGLAND.
Stone over stone, over the shaking track,
They start their journey: jarring muscle and aching
Back crunch the fading county into
Dust. Stone over stone, over the trundling
Mile, they stumble and trudge: where the thirsty bramble
Begs at the sleeve, the pot-hole tugs the foot.
Stone over stone, over the trampled sunlight,
Over the flagging day, over the burn
And blister of the dry boot, they flog their way
To where the journeyless and roofless trees
Muster against the plunging of the dark:
Where the shut door and the ministering fire
Have shrunk across the fields to a dog's bark,

To a charred circle in the grass.
No floorboard mouse, no tattling friend; only
The flickering bat dodging the night air,
Only the stoat clapping the fern as it runs.

Stone over stone, Cuthman has spoken out
His faith to his mother. She has been comforted
A little; begins to believe in her son.
He has made her clumsy rhymes to laugh at.
She has tried to tell him stories of his grandmother,
But it is hard to talk buffeted by a cart.

After these miles, at last when the day leans
On the wall, at last when the vagrant hour flops
In the shade, they found a protected place, a ground
Where limbs and prayers could stretch between root and
Root, between root and sky; and they slept under curfew
Or Cuthman slept. His mother was chasing fears
Until daylight. 'What is rustling in the grass?
What shakes in the tree? What is hiding in
The shadow?' And Cuthman said, 'God is there.
God is waiting with us.'

Stone over stone, in the thin morning, they plod
Again, until they come to a field where mowers
Sweep their scythes under the dry sun.

                    [*The* MOWERS *at work in the field. They sing.*

MOWERS. The muscle and the meadow
               Make men sing,
           And the grass grows high
           Like lashes to a lady's eye.
           Sickle-blades go sliding by
               And so does everything,
           Grass, the year, and a merry friend
               All at last come to an end.

Enter CUTHMAN *wheeling his* MOTHER. *The* MOWERS *stop work and nudge each other.*

MOTHER. I have gone up and down stairs fifty times a day when you were a baby and your aunt lived with us. She was an invalid but you wouldn't remember her. I have dug in the garden for your father, and had all the housework to do into the bargain. You don't know the work there is to do in a house. Your father's brother came to see us (you were only two months old at the time) and he said: 'Sister, you must be made of rope. My wife has help in the house, but nevertheless when she takes a broom in her hand she bursts into tears.' And I wasn't young, you must remember. I was nearly forty years old when I married your father. But never mind that. The point is that we've come a long way, so far that it's a wonder we've still kept the sun in sight; and I've been so jogged and jerked that I think your uncle must have been right. I begin to think that I'm really made of rope.

[*At this moment the rope round* CUTHMAN'S *shoulders breaks, and his mother is rolled on to the ground. The* MOWERS *burst out laughing.*

CUTHMAN. Are you hurt, Mother? The rope broke. How are you, Mother, are you all right?

MOTHER. Oh! Oh! If your mother ever walks again you'll be luckier than you deserve. This is what it has come to. You bring me all these miles to throw me on the ground.

CUTHMAN. The rope broke, Mother. Are you hurt?

MOTHER. Of course I'm hurt. I'm more than hurt, I'm injured.

CUTHMAN. Let me help you up; see if you can walk.

MOTHER. Walk? I might as well try to fly. What are all those people laughing at?

CUTHMAN. Try to stand on your legs.

MOTHER. They're laughing at me; that's what's the matter with

them. They're laughing at an old woman who has had a misfortune. I told you what kind of place the world was, Cuthman, and
I shall put a stop to it. I tell you, I've a sense of humour, but I
won't be laughed at. [*She gets to her feet and rounds on the*
MOWERS.] I don't know who you are, but I'm glad I wasn't born
in your part of the country. Where I was born we knew how to
behave; we knew better than to laugh at an old woman who had
come to grief. We were very respected in the village where we
come from, I may tell you; but as it happens we decided to travel.
[*The* MOWERS *give an even louder roar of laughter.*] All right, all
right! One of these days you'll laugh for too long, you'll laugh
yourselves into trouble, take my word for it.

CUTHMAN. I must make a new rope for the cart; I shall have to
make it out of withies. We shall find some at the stream we just
passed over, remember, Mother? Fifty yards back or so. What
will you do? Would you rather stay here, or come with me?

1ST MOWER. Did you hear what the boy said? A rope of withies!
What a joke!

2ND MOWER. Don't you go and make the rope too strong, baby
boy. You needn't go further than the end of the earth to find a
fortune!

[*They go off again into a roar of laughter.*

MOTHER. I should like to box the ears of the whole lot, but there
are too many of them; it would take too long.

CUTHMAN. Let's go, Mother; let's find the withies.

MOTHER. I may be lame, but I'd walk away from this place if it
was the last thing I did.

[*They go off,* CUTHMAN *wheeling the cart.*

3RD MOWER [*singing after them*].
　　　Don't fall into the stream, Mother.
　　　The water's very high.
　　　We might not hear you scream, Mother
　　　And we'd hate to see you die!

[*They laugh again, and sing it all together.*

4TH MOWER. Here, did you feel that? A drop of rain!

1ST MOWER. Never; never on your life.

4TH MOWER. I swear it was. I felt a drop of rain. Look at the clouds coming up.

2ND MOWER. He's right. I felt a drop on my hand, and another, and another!

3RD MOWER. Don't stand about then. For the crop's sake, get at the hay!

[They feverishly set to work.

1ST MOWER. It's no good. We can do nothing at all—the whole sky is opening.

THE PEOPLE OF SOUTH ENGLAND.
That is rain on dry ground. We heard it:
We saw the little tempest in the grass,
The panic of anticipation: heard
The uneasy leaves flutter, the air pass
In a wave, the fluster of the vegetation;

Heard the first spatter of drops, the outriders
Larruping on the road, hitting against
The gate of the drought, and shattering
On to the lances of the tottering meadow
It is rain; it is rain on dry ground.

Rain riding suddenly out of the air,
Battering the bare walls of the sun.
It is falling on to the tongue of the blackbird,
Into the heart of the thrush; the dazed valley
Sings it down. Rain, rain on dry ground!

This is the urgent decision of the day,
The urgent drubbing of earth, the urgent raid
On the dust; downpour over the flaring poppy,
Deluge on the face of noon, the flagellant
Rain drenching across the air.—The day

Flows in the ditch; bubble and twisting twig
And the sodden morning swirl along together
Under the crying hedge. And where the sun
Ran on the scythes, the rain runs down
The obliterated field, the blunted crop.

[*The* MOWERS *have fled from the rain, leaving the hay to
disaster.*

THE PEOPLE OF SOUTH ENGLAND.
The rain stops.
The air is sprung with green.
The intercepted drops
Fall at their leisure; and between
The threading runnels on the slopes
The snail drags his caution into the sun.

Re-enter CUTHMAN *and his* MOTHER, *his rope of withies
fastened from the cart to his shoulder.*

CUTHMAN. All the mowers are gone.

MOTHER. If I'd been the ground under their feet I should have
swallowed the lot.

CUTHMAN. But look at the field! You might think the sky had
crashed on to it.

MOTHER. Rain! I never!

CUTHMAN. Down by the stream there wasn't even a shower; we
had a hard job keeping the sun out of our eyes. But here the
crop is ruined and everywhere is running with water. Only a
field away, and we felt nothing of it!

MOTHER. They were laughing at an old woman come to grief. I
told them how it would be. You'll go on laughing too long, I said.
And look what a plight they're in now.—Poor souls.

CUTHMAN. Mother—

MOTHER. What is it, son?

CUTHMAN. When the withies break—

MOTHER. What! When the withies break! Do you think I'll get back into that cart when I shall be expecting every bump to be my last? You don't know your mother, Cuthman. She doesn't walk up to misfortune like a horse to sugar.

CUTHMAN. I shall be ready for it this time, Mother.

MOTHER. So you will, and so shall I. My eyes will be round your neck every minute of the day.

CUTHMAN. I shall look out and keep a good hold on the handles. And when the withies break——

MOTHER. If you can tell me what happens then it will be a relief to me.

CUTHMAN. We won't go any further.

MOTHER. That's just what I was afraid of. All my bones will be broken to smithereens.

CUTHMAN. When we had gone down to the banks of the stream
And were cutting willow-shoots (listen, Mother,
This is something I must tell you: how
From today for all my days life has to be,
How life is proving) while the rain was falling
Behind us in the field though we still wore
The sun like a coat, I felt the mood
Of the meadow change, as though a tide
Had turned in the sap, or heaven from the balance
Of creation had shifted a degree.
The skirling water crept into a flow,
The sapling flickered in my hand, timber
And flesh seemed of equal and old significance.
At that place, and then, I tell you, Mother,
God rode up my spirit and drew in
Beside me. His breath met on my breath, moved
And mingled. I was taller then than death.
Under the willows I was taller than death.

B

MOTHER. I saw you standing quiet. I said to myself
He has something in his heart, he has something
That occupies him.

CUTHMAN.   We shall go as far
As the withies take us. There, where they break,
Where God breaks them, you shall set up
House again and put clean paper on
Larder shelves. And there where God breaks them
And scoops our peace out of a strange field
I shall build my answer in plank and brick,
Labour out my thanks in plaster and beam
And stone. You, Mother, and I, when God
Brings our settled days again, will build
A church where the withies are broken, a church to pray in
When you have put your broom away, and untied
Your apron.

MOTHER.   Build a church, with our own hands?

CUTHMAN. With our own hands, Mother, and with our own
Love of God and with nothing else; for I have
Nothing else; I have no craft or knowledge of joint
Or strain, more than will make a cart, and even
The cart you scarcely would call handsome. What
Did I learn to do after I found my feet
And found my tongue? Only to seem as intelligent
As the neighbours' children whatever happened; to be
Always a little less than myself in order
To avoid being conspicuous. But now
I am less than I would be, less
Than I must be; my buzzing life is less
Than my birth was or my death will be. The church
And I shall be built together; and together
Find our significance. Breaking and building
In the progression of this world go hand in hand.
And where the withies break I shall build.

MOTHER. I am always lagging a little behind your thoughts,
  I am always put out of breath by them. No doubt
  I shall arrive one of these days.
CUTHMAN.   In, Mother.
  We shall arrive together if the cart holds good.
MOTHER. It always seems to me I take my life
  In my hands, every time I get into this
  Contraption.
CUTHMAN.   Listen to that! A hard week's work
  And she calls it a contraption!

                                   [*They set out again.*
THE PEOPLE OF SOUTH ENGLAND.
            For the lifetime of a sapling-rope
            Plaited in the eye of God,
            Among the unfamiliar twine
            Of England, he still must strain
            And plug the uneasy slope,
            And struggle in heavy sun, and plod
            Out his vision; still must haunt
            Along the evening battlement
            Of hills and creep in the long valleys
            In the insect's trail, the small the dogged
            Pinhead of dust, by whose desire
            A church shall struggle into the air.
            No flattering builder of follies
            Would lay foundations so deep and rugged
            A church, a church will branch at last
            Above a country pentecost,
            And the vision at last will find its people
            And the prayers at last be said.
            This is how he mutters and how
            Weariness runs off his brow.
            Already the bell climbs in the steeple,
            The belfry of his shaggy head,

And the choir over and over again
Sings in the chancel of his brain.
Across the shorn downs, to the foot,
To Steyning, the last laborious track
Is trapesed and the withies at his neck
Untwist and break.
So he tips the stone from his boot,
Laughs at the smoking stack,
At the carthorse shaking its brass,
And knows the evening will turn a friendly face.

Enter TAWM, *an old man. He keeps a look-out over his shoulder.*

TAWM. They'll be after me again, not a corner of Steyning but they'll ferret me out; my daughter and my daughter's husband and my daughter's daughter; my nephew and my nephew's nephews: they'll be after me. 'There's a cold wind, Father (or uncle or grandfather or whatever it is); take care of yourself, wrap yourself up; it's going to rain, it's likely to snow, there's a heavy dew.' What do they think I was born into this world for if it wasn't to die of it?

VOICES [*off stage*]. Father! Father!

TAWM. The ferrets, the ferrets! If I climbed up on to a cloud they'd find me out and bring me my hat.

Enter his DAUGHTER *and his* SON-IN-LAW.

DAUGHTER. Father, whatever are you thinking about? Why ever do you want to go walking about the fields with a cold wind blowing? I've got your supper waiting for you.

SON-IN-LAW. Here's your hat.

TAWM [*with bitterness*]. Daughter, your husband's a most obliging man. He brings me my hat when the wind's in my hair. Thank you, son; you're an invaluable fellow.

Enter CUTHMAN *wheeling his* MOTHER.

DAUGHTER. Who ever have we got here?   [*She giggles.*

SON-IN-LAW. They're nobody I know. I've seen everybody twenty miles around and this is none of them.

TAWM. They're strangers, likely as not. If I was challenged I shouldn't be afraid to say that these are strangers.

DAUGHTER. What does he think he's doing going around like that with the old woman? I've never seen anything like it.

[*She giggles again.*

TAWM. You've got no understanding of geography, daughter. All the places in the world have their own ways and this young man is doing so because it's his way.

MOTHER. Cuthman, this is a very pretty place, quite a picture. The beauties of nature always make me feel honest with myself.

CUTHMAN. Mother, the withies have broken!

MOTHER. I remember when I was a girl I went up to my mother with a bunch of cornflowers in my hand—

CUTHMAN. Mother, the withies! The withies have broken!

MOTHER. Nothing has happened to me; I'm still where I was; I'm still in the cart.

CUTHMAN. I was holding it firm; but look at them, they've chafed in two. You can get out of it now, Mother; we're not going any further.

MOTHER. If ever I sit in a chair again I shan't recognize myself. What a very pretty place! Are we really stopping here, Cuthman?

CUTHMAN. Yes, Mother; we've arrived.

MOTHER. It's too much to believe all in a minute. But one thing's quite certain: it'll be a good many nights before I stop bumping about in my dreams.

[*A crowd of* VILLAGERS *has collected. They stare at* CUTHMAN *and his* MOTHER.

CUTHMAN. Why do you think all these people are staring, Mother?

MOTHER. They're welcoming us. It's like old times. It was just like this when your father brought me home on the back of his horse.

CUTHMAN [*calling out to them*]. Could you tell me the name of this place, please?

> [*The* VILLAGERS *continue to stare.*

CUTHMAN. I say! Would you mind telling us where we are?—They're dumb, Mother.

MOTHER. They like us and respect us. One of these days they'll tell us so. It was just like this when your father brought me home, and they told me afterwards they liked the look of me at once they said.

TAWM. Good evening.

CUTHMAN. Good evening.

MOTHER. Good evening.

TAWM. Can I be of any help to you at all?

CUTHMAN. Perhaps you could tell us the name of this place.

TAWM. P'r'aps I could. I've lived here seventy years, so p'r'aps I could. It's Steyning, if I remember right.

CUTHMAN. Steyning . . . The church at Steyning.

TAWM. The church? If that's what you're after you've got the wrong place; there's no church here.

A WOMAN. This is a poor place and we're poor people; we must pray on the bare ground.

CUTHMAN. I've come to build a church.

> [*This causes a sensation among the* VILLAGERS.

MOTHER. It's an idea that my boy has; he has got it very much at heart. But I don't know what we can be looking like; I can't imagine at all. You must take us for tramps. Before my husband died I always hoped that one day we'd see the country together, but it really is very tiring. Some one ought to do something about the state of the roads. My husband was a farmer.

TAWM. Does the boy want work to do?

CUTHMAN. Yes, I do.

TAWM. How does he treat you, Mother? Does he pester you with shawls for your shoulders to keep the air off, with hats and over-shoes and gloves? Eh, does he? Does he protect you from draughts and shade you from the sun and hurry you out of the rain?

MOTHER. Listen, my goodness me! He asks me that, when he can see for himself how it is. My son pushes me into a cart and bumps and bangs me a million miles until I am the colour of midnight. And then he tips me out on to the hard ground as though I was refuse. And then into the cart I go again and over the hills, with the sun on me and the rain on me, and snow would have been all the same if it had come. But he is a good boy and his singing voice has improved wonderfully on the journey.

TAWM. He's a credit to you, Mother, and I shall borrow him from you when the need arises. We must find him work to do. My son is a good son, too, but he has gone off to the city. He wasn't a ferret either. Here's the farmer coming along that he was shepherd to. He'll be short-handed without my boy. [*To* CUTH-MAN.] Can you manage sheep?

CUTHMAN. I looked after them for my father.

MOTHER. He's a great lover of animals, aren't you, Cuthman? And, as I say to him, animals know. Even sheep know. He can do anything he likes with them.

[*The* FARMER *comes up to them.*

FARMER. Good evening, Tawm.

TAWM. You'll be needing another hand, I shouldn't be surprised, now that my son has gone scrimshanking off to the city.

FARMER. It's a loss, Tawm, and a pity he couldn't settle himself down like anyone else. Work's heavy enough at this time of year without being hobbled by a man short.

TAWM. Never in all my years, Mister, have I known a time when young men were scarcer.

FARMER. That's true, Tawm; there never has been such a time.

TAWM. I've been thinking, Mister; there's a young man here might do you fine. He's just such a one as my son was. He knows the difference between a man and a piece of flimsy.

FARMER [*to* CUTHMAN]. Are you a shepherd, son?

CUTHMAN. Yes, sir; I was shepherd for my father.

FARMER. Strangers, eh?

CUTHMAN. Yes, sir; strangers.

FARMER. Well, you've come at a good time. We can do with you. Is this your mother?

MOTHER. I'm his mother and there's one thing in the world I need, and that's a cushion at my back. Give me a rest and I shall begin to understand that good fortune's come our way at last.

TAWM. You can think yourself lucky, Mother, that life isn't for ever shoving a footstool under your feet.

FARMER. Come back to my house with me; we'll talk about this. There's a pot of stew on the fire that I shall be eating for three days if I can't find some one to help me out with it.

DAUGHTER [*to* TAWM]. Father, come in do. Your supper will be spoiled and you'll be in bed tomorrow with this dew soaking into your feet.

TAWM [*to* MOTHER]. You see how it is, neighbour; you see how it is.

MOTHER. It is just like old times to hear you calling me Neighbour; everything is most delightful.

CUTHMAN. I'll fetch the cart and catch you up.

[*Exeunt Omnes, except* CUTHMAN, *who goes to the cart.*

You see what comfort you have brought to us,
Old rough and ready! But your work's not over.

Those others have already forgotten the church
I've come to build, or find it hard to believe.
But when creation's tide crawled on its first
Advance across the sand of the air, and earth
Tossed its tentative hills, this place of idle
Grass where we are idling took the imprint
Of a dedication, which interminable
History could not weather away. And now
The consummation climbs on to the hill:
A church where the sun will beat on the bell, a church
To hold in its sanctuary the last light.
God be on the hill, and in my heart
And hand. God guide the hammer and the plane.
As the root is guided. Let there be a church—

> [*He grips the handles of the cart.*

Come on now, rough and ready.

> [*Exit* CUTHMAN *with the cart.*

Enter two brothers, ALFRED *and* DEMIWULF, *the sons of*
MRS. FIPPS, *who later will give her name to Fippa's Pit:*
Fippa Puteus.

ALFRED. A fat lot of good it is mooching about with a scowl on
your face. It only makes you look like a sick dog. We must make
the place too hot to hold him; there's nothing else for it.

DEMIWULF. So we will, so we certainly will! I'll make sure he
goes off with a flea in his ear!—

ALFRED. Well, let's see you. He's been here a week and you've
done precious little so far, except grind your teeth.

DEMIWULF. That's all you know. I've been speaking to people
about it.

ALFRED. And what good's that, I'd like to know? What earthly
good is it? Nobody has any ears for anyone except this ninny
hammer of a boy. There's no sociability in the village any longer,

that's what I say. Nobody ever comes to play bowls on Saturday evenings. We can't even put up a shove-ha'penny team against Bramber. Nobody can think of anything except this crazy idea of building a church.

DEMIWULF. They're a lot of gooseheads; they're a set of nincompoops, all of them, the whole lot of them! There's not a body in the village that hasn't been bitten by it, except we two and mother.

ALFRED. The farmer has given him the ground.

DEMIWULF. The builder has given him the bricks.

ALFRED. The woodman has given him the timber.

DEMIWULF. Everybody is making a fool of himself in his own way.

ALFRED. Except we two and mother.

DEMIWULF. Let's walk over to Bramber. I'm sick of the whole thing.

[*Exeunt.*

THE PEOPLE OF SOUTH ENGLAND.
Let time rely on the regular interval
Of days, but we do no such thing. We pull
Down the weeks and months like a bough of cherry
To decorate our room: strip off the year
As lightly as we tear off the forgotten
Calendar. But the story must be told.
We make a country dance of Cuthman's labours
And widely separated days become near neighbours.

Enter CUTHMAN'S MOTHER *wearing a white apron.*

MOTHER. It's an astonishing thing how time flies. It only seems yesterday that I was being bounced all over the world, and now we've been settled in Steyning for six months as though we had lived here all our lives. Every one has been very kind. Cuthman is earning quite good money from the gentleman we met on the first evening we came. We live in a very nice little cottage. There are rather too many steps but one can't expect everything. Every day I put on a clean apron and the neighbours tell me that they liked the look of me at once. We are already very respected. And it is really wonderful the way everybody helps my son with his church. Every spare moment they have they go with him and do a little more. Besides giving the field, the gentleman we met on the first evening has also given two oxen to help with the work. I told Cuthman that I thought it was extremely generous and he ought to feel very fortunate. When I have finished my work I go down to the church and watch all the villagers singing and hammering in the cool of the day. . . . Well, I must now draw to a close. I have some milk on the fire and by this time it will probably all be boiled over. [*Exit.*

Enter CUTHMAN, *dragging behind him an oxen-yoke. Enter to him* ALFRED *and* DEMIWULF.

CUTHMAN. Good afternoon, neighbours.

[*The* BROTHERS *pass by without speaking.*

CUTHMAN. Could you tell me—have you seen my oxen?

ALFRED [*to* DEMIWULF]. Was the boy speaking to us?

DEMIWULF. I think he was. Something about oxen.

ALFRED [*to* CUTHMAN]. Are you wanting something?

CUTHMAN. My two oxen have strayed away somewhere. They're working with us on the church and we're needing them. Have you seen them anywhere about?

ALFRED. Not a sign. We've seen two oxen belonging to your master.

CUTHMAN. My master gave them to me for the work of the church. Where did you see them?

DEMIWULF. They were on our land.

ALFRED. Trespassing.

DEMIWULF. So we shut them up.

CUTHMAN. I'm sorry they were trespassing. I'll see in future that they stay where they belong. If you could fetch them for me I'll put them to work.

ALFRED. Oh no.

DEMIWULF. Oh no. They stay where they are.

CUTHMAN. We need them.

ALFRED. Then it's a pity you let them go plunging about on other people's property.

DEMIWULF. Where they are they'll stay, and that's flat.

CUTHMAN. What purpose will they serve shut up in a barn? We need them for the building.

ALFRED. So we heard you say.

CUTHMAN. There's one thing that I'll not see any man destroy; there's one fire in me that no man shall put out. I am dangerous as I stand over the foundations of the church. I have the unsleeping eyes of a watch-dog.

DEMIWULF. Go and yoke yourself. No doubt you'll find somebody who'll be only too pleased to drive you.

CUTHMAN. I ask you again: Let me have those oxen.

ALFRED. I'm sorry. I'm afraid there's nothing we can do about it.

CUTHMAN. Then I must move. One day I took a crook
And drew a circle in pasture; and today
I draw a circle here to guard the church,
A circle of a stronger faith than I
Could ever have mastered then. Already you slough
Your little spite; it has deserted you,
And all your power to stir and strength to speak
Has fallen round your ankles, where it hangs
With the weight of chain. And you are naked
Without your fashion of malice, and dumb without
Your surly tongues. But you shall help with the church

Since you refuse the oxen. You shall have
Their glory.

[*He yokes them together. As he does so the* NEIGHBOURS
enter and stand a little way off.

1ST NEIGHBOUR. Look what Cuthman is doing!

2ND NEIGHBOUR. Look! He is yoking them!

OTHERS. Can he be joking? Is this in fun?
They would never permit. They'd never allow
Liberties for the sake of a laugh.
He is angry. He is driving them
As though they were shallow-skulls,
As though they were thick-skins,
As though they were beasts of the field.

1ST NEIGHBOUR. It is neither anger nor fun.
It is the same stress that we see
Knotting his forearm and kneading his forehead
To drops of sweat when he wrestles
With timber in the framework of the church.

2ND NEIGHBOUR. What will their mother have to say about it?

MRS. FIPPS [*bursting through the crowd*].
I'll show you what their mother will have to say!
What's come over you all to stand and gape,
With outrage running to seed under your eyes?
Do you want all our days to be choked with insults
And devilment? We've stood a lot too much
Nonsense from this canting baby,
A lot too much.

[*To* CUTHMAN.] Take that off the backs of my sons and get out of
this place. Do you hear me? Get out of this place! Take it off, I
tell you! And don't let me see you or your amiable mother skulking
round these parts any longer. Do you hear what I say?

CUTHMAN. Wait a moment. Your sons have shut up the oxen that
were helping with the church. I asked them to give them back to

us, but that's something they're not prepared to do. The building
shall not be interrupted. If they'll not return the oxen they must
replace them.

MRS. FIPPS. You overbearing little brat! You'll be shut up yourself if I have anything to do with it; I'll see to it! I'll put you and
your mother on the way where you belong—in the ditch with
vagrants! My poor Alfred, my poor Demiwulf, your mother will
see that the nasty wicked boy doesn't hurt you. . . . It's your
mother talking to you. Alfred! Demiwulf! Can't you hear me?—
You've murdered them on their legs, that's what you've done.
Take that thing off their backs before I get my hands to you. Go
on! You insolent bantam! Do what I say! . . . [*A change comes
over her.*] What's happening? I'm being pushed over! I'm being
knocked down!

NEIGHBOURS. What a wind has got up! What a gale!

MRS. FIPPS. Help! Help! The wind is blowing me over!

NEIGHBOURS. Mind your heads! The chimneys will be off!
What a tornado!

MRS. FIPPS. Help! It's whirling me round!
It'll have me off my feet!

NEIGHBOURS. It will have her down!
Look at her, look at her now!

MRS. FIPPS. Help! Help!

[*The wind blows her out of sight.*

THE PEOPLE OF SOUTH ENGLAND.
The arms of the wood were not ready for this,
The turbulent boy who has pitched himself suddenly in,
The headlong ruffian hurling himself in the lap
Of the valley:
What can protect us from this ragamuffin
Who has stampeded into his manhood with
The shudder of the first anger of a rocket?
He has slammed back the ocean's stable-doors

And slapped the sturdy bases of the earth,
Wrenched and worried into the heart of heaven
And dragged a bellowing Lucifer to ground.
He has belaboured the homeflight of the day
Into a staggered bird. The word's gone round:
There will be no quarter, no pouring of oil.
The roots clutch in the soil, frantic against
The sobbing of the bough. The gates of evening
Clang in vain. Darkness will topple down
Under the guns of the enormous air.
It has lifted an old woman off her feet!
This is a matter of considerable local interest.
It is carrying her up as high as the trees,
Zigzag like a paper bag, like somebody's hat!
There hasn't been a hurricane like this
In living memory. It only shows
How ludicrous it is to strut in a storm.
Zigzag like a paper bag, like somebody's hat!
It will be a long time before we have exhausted
All the possibilities of a story
As amazing as this one is. Up! Up! Up!

NEIGHBOURS. Up! Up! Up!

[*The* NEIGHBOURS *with shrieks and squeals rush off to follow the old woman's flight.*

THE PEOPLE OF SOUTH ENGLAND.
You may not think it possible, but tradition
Has it that this old woman was carried five
Miles and dropped in a pond. It's scarcely
Credible, but that is the story that got
About. And when the hurricane had dropped her
It dropped itself and the incident was closed.

CUTHMAN [*unyoking the* BROTHERS]. Well that was an upheaval.
You'd better go and look for your mother. She'll be some way
off by this time.

ALFRED. I'm not feeling very well. It's as though I was conva-
lescing after a long illness. My voice seems to be climbing back
on my tongue.

DEMIWULF. I feel like a toad crawling out from under a stone

CUTHMAN. Before you do anything else perhaps you would fetch
the oxen for me? It's time we got busy with them.

ALFRED. We'll fetch them for you at once.

DEMIWULF. At once. We're sorry if you have been put to any inconvenience.

CUTHMAN. The inconvenience was mutual. I shall be at the church.

[*Exit* CUTHMAN.

ALFRED [*as he and his brother go off*]. I wonder where mother is by
now? She always disliked long journeys, but at any rate she
hasn't got any luggage to worry about.

THE PEOPLE OF SOUTH ENGLAND.
Do you catch the time of the tune that the shepherd plays
Under the irregular bough of the oak-tree,
The tune of the tale he expects your brain to dance to,
The time of the tune as irregular as the bough?
It will not come as anything fresh to you
That instead of events keeping their proper stations
They are huddling together as though to find protection
From rain that spoils the mowers' crop
From wind sweeping old women off their feet.
We merely remind you, though we've told you before,
How things stand. We're apt to take the meticulous
Intervention of the sun, the strict
Moon and the seasons much too much for granted.

Enter CUTHMAN'S MOTHER *and* TAWM. *Enter to them some*
of the NEIGHBOURS, *downcast.*

MOTHER. I can hardly wait for my son to know. He has already
grown to love you like a father, I know that; he has often told me

so. It is nearly two years since we first met. How astonishing, two years! Do you remember how we arrived with that dreadful cart? I was so ashamed. You must have thought we were nothing but riff-raff, and little did I imagine what was in store for us. Usually my intuition is most acute; things say themselves to me. But oddly enough nothing said to me 'One day that dear man is going to be your husband,' nothing at all.—Here are some of the neighbours coming from the church. It's getting on so nicely. Good evening, neighbours. Is it nearly done?

1ST NEIGHBOUR. It'll never be done.

2ND NEIGHBOUR. It'll never be finished now.

1ST NEIGHBOUR. There'll be no church.

MOTHER. Never be finished? Tush and nonsense! What creatures men are. You're up to the roof.

1ST NEIGHBOUR. Up to the roof we may be but we'll get no further. The king-post has beaten us.

TAWM. You can't be beaten by a piece of timber; it isn't princely in a man to be beaten by a piece of timber.

MOTHER. Listen to what he says and be ashamed of yourselves. We are old, this dear man and I, and we know what is right.

1ST NEIGHBOUR. The work was almost done, and then someone suddenly shouted 'The king-post has swung out of position!' It had set other places wrong, that had been ready. For days we have laboured at it, and as time went on we laboured and prayed, but nothing will make it go into its place. We're not knowledgeable men with these things. It's not our work and a church isn't like a little cottage. We've none of the proper appurtenances for the job. There's no hope for it, even if we go on trying till we're whiteheaded.

MOTHER. But Cuthman—he thinks of nothing but how the building grows, nothing but of the day when it will be done—where is he? What is he doing?

2ND NEIGHBOUR. We couldn't get him away. For days he has
tugged and tusselled with us, with the blood in his face and the
veins pushing in his head. And now he has gone into a ghost.
He smoothes the stone with his hand as though it were in a fever
and sleepless. He pats it as though it were a horse that had brought
him safely through battle. And then he stands heavily in the aisle
with his misery staring to the east.

MOTHER. Poor Cuthman, poor sweet son! On our journey it was
ahead of him like riches, and every moment of his holiday time
he has run to it as though he had heaven at his shoulders. This
will damage him. I'm afraid for him and I don't mind telling you.

TAWM. Here's the boy; here he is.

Enter CUTHMAN *running. Other* NEIGHBOURS *join the group.*

MOTHER. Cuthman, what has happened to you? Son,
What is the matter?

CUTHMAN.   The king-post is in place
Again! The church will be finished.

MOTHER.   But the neighbours
Said there was no one with you. You were alone.

CUTHMAN. I was alone by the unattended pillar,
Mourning the bereaved air that lay so quiet
Between walls; hungry for hammer-blows.
And the momentous hive that once was there.
And when I prayed my voice slid to the ground
Like a crashed pediment.
There was a demolition written over
The walls, and dogs rummaged in the foundations,
And picnic parties laughed on a heap of stone.
But gradually I was aware of some one in
The doorway and turned my eyes that way and saw
Carved out of the sunlight a man who stood
Watching me, so still that there was not
Other such stillness anywhere on the earth,

So still that the air seemed to leap
At his side. He came towards me, and the sun
Flooded its banks and flowed across the shadow.
He asked me why I stood alone. His voice
Hovered on memory with open wings
And drew itself up from a chine of silence
As though it had longtime lain in a vein of gold.
I told him: It is the king-post.
He stretched his hand upon it. At his touch
It lifted to its place. There was no sound.
I cried out, and I cried at last 'Who are you?'
I heard him say 'I was a carpenter' . . .

                        [They fall upon their knees.

There under the bare walls of our labour
Death and life were knotted in one strength
Indivisible as root and sky.

THE PEOPLE OF SOUTH ENGLAND.
The candle of our story has burnt down
And Cuthman's life is puffed like a dandelion
Into uncertain places. But the hand
Still leads the earth to drink at the sky, and still
The messenger rides into the city of leaves
Under the gradual fires of September;
The Spring shall hear, the Winter shall be wise
To warning of aconite and freezing lily,
And all shall watch the augur of a star
And learn their stillness from a stiller heaven.
And what of us who upon Cuthman's world
Have grafted progress without lock or ratchet?
What of us who have to catch up, always
To catch up with the high-powered car, or with
The unbalanced budget, to cope with competition,
To weather the sudden thunder of the uneasy
Frontier? We also loom with the earth

Over the waterways of space. Between
Our birth and death we may touch understanding
As a moth brushes a window with its wing.

Who shall question then
Why we lean our bicycle against a hedge
And go into the house of God?
Who shall question
That coming out from our doorways
We have discerned a little, we have known
More than the gossip that comes to us over our gates.

THE FIRSTBORN

A Play in Three Acts

THIRD EDITION

To

MY MOTHER
and
MY BROTHER

FOREWORD
TO THE SECOND EDITION

THIS play—begun as long ago as 1938, though not finished until 1945 after four years when circumstance made me neglect it—has a title which at first may seem to quarrel with most of the action, since the chief protagonist is Moses. But I hope, after a little acquaintance, the figure of life which Rameses presents will be seen to take a central place from his first entrance to the end. The character of Moses is a movement towards maturity, towards a balancing of life within the mystery, where the conflicts and dilemmas are the trembling of the balance. In the last scene he suffers a momentary spiritual death ('I followed a light into a blindness') at the moment when the firstborn's physical death creates the Hebrews' freedom; and his resurrection from that, to become the great leader, though only hinted at as the curtain falls, carries with it something of the life of Rameses.

> Death was their question to us, and our lives
> Become their understanding or perplexity.
> And by living to answer them, we also answer
> Our own impermanence.

Rameses lives a boyhood almost identical with Moses' own; he and the Hebrew Shendi between them draw the frontiers of combat altogether differently from the lines laid down by accepted human action. Rameses is the innocence, humanity, vigour, and worth which stand on the enemy side, not altering the justice or necessity of Moses' cause, but linking the ways of men and the ways of God with a deep and urgent question-mark.

I made certain alterations and cuts immediately after the Edinburgh Festival production in 1948; and for this edition I have revised those alterations, refashioned the last scene, and cut further. This is a welcome opportunity to say how much I was helped, in the play's early stages, by the encouragement of Gerard Hopkins and the late Charles Williams; and by Frank Kendon, of the Cambridge University Press, whose belief in it, in 1946, first saw it into print.

C. F.

28 *December* 1951

This edition of *The Firstborn* incorporates alterations which I made for the New York production (April 1958) which, later in the same year, visited Tel Aviv on the occasion of the tenth anniversary of the founding of the State of Israel.

A play can be a fairly fluid affair, taking new turns in the hands of different actors. In making the present version I was much helped by the imaginative penetration of Anthony Quayle who both played the part of Moses and directed the production.

C. F.

June 1958

Gateway Theatre, Edinburgh, 6 *September* 1948

Anath Bithiah	ATHENE SEYLER
Teusret	DEIRDRE DOONE
Seti the Second	ROBERT SPEAIGHT
Rameses	PAUL HANSARD
Moses	IVAN BRANDT
Aaron	ROBERT SANSOM
Miriam	HENZIE RAEBURN
Shendi	ROBERT RIETTY

Directed by E. Martin Browne

Winter Garden Theatre, London, 29 *January* 1952

Anath Bithiah	BARBARA EVEREST
Teusret	RUTH TROUNCER
Seti the Second	MARK DIGNAM
Rameses	TONY BRITTON
Moses	ALEC CLUNES
Aaron	CYRIL LUCKHAM
Miriam	DOROTHY REYNOLDS
Shendi	ROBERT RIETTY

Directed by John Fernald

Coronet Theatre, New York, 30 *April* 1958

Anath Bithiah	KATHARINE CORNELL
Teusret	KATHLEEN WIDDOES
Seti the Second	TORIN THATCHER
Rameses	ROBERT DRIVAS
Moses	ANTHONY QUAYLE
Aaron	MICHAEL STRONG
Miriam	MILDRED NATWICK
Shendi	MICHAEL WAGER

Directed by Anthony Quayle

CHARACTERS

IN THE ORDER OF THEIR APPEARANCE

ANATH BITHIAH, *Pharaoh's sister*
TEUSRET, *Pharaoh's daughter*
SETI THE SECOND, *the Pharaoh*
RAMESES, *his son*
MOSES
AARON, *his brother*
MIRIAM, *his sister*
SHENDI, *Miriam's son*
Two overseers, a Minister (KEF)
A guard and a servant

*The action of the play takes place in
the summer of 1200 B.C., alternating
between Pharaoh's palace and
Miriam's tent*

ACT ONE

SCENE ONE

*The terrace of the palace of Seti the Second, at Tanis. A morning in the
summer of* 1200 B.C. *A flight of steps (unseen) leads down through a gate
to open ground. The terrace looks out upon an incompleted pyramid.*

A scream.

Enter from the palace ANATH BITHIAH, *a woman of fifty, sister to the
Pharaoh, and* TEUSRET, *a girl of fifteen, the Pharaoh's daughter*

ANATH. What was it, Teusret?

TEUSRET.   Did you hear it too?

ANATH. Some man is dead. That scream was password to a grave.
   Look there: up go the birds!

TEUSRET.   The heat on this terrace!
   You could bake on these stones, Aunt Anath.

ANATH.   Ask who it was.

TEUSRET. They're working steadily at father's tomb.
   There's no sign of trouble.

ANATH.   We're too far off to see.
   We should know more if we could see their faces.

TEUSRET [*calling down the steps*]. Guard! Come up here.

ANATH.   I should like to be certain.
   Oh, that pyramid! Everyday, watching it build,
   Will make an old woman of me early.
   It will cast a pretty shadow when it's done.
   Two hundred more men were taken on today,
   Did you know that, Teusret? Your father's in a hurry.

(55)

Their sweat would be invaluable to the farmers in this drought.
What pains they take to house a family of dust.

TEUSRET. It's a lovely tomb.

ANATH.   Yes, so it may be.
But what shall we do with all that air to breathe
And no more breath? I could as happily lie
And wait for eternal life in something smaller.

Enter A GUARD

TEUSRET. What was that scream we heard?

GUARD.   It's nothing, madam.

ANATH. You are right. Nothing. It was something once
But now it is only a scare of birds in the air
And a pair of women with their nerves uncovered;
Nothing.

TEUSRET. Who was it screamed?

GUARD.   One of the builders
Missed his footing, madam; merely an Israelite.
They're digging him into the sand. No, over to the left.

TEUSRET. Oh yes, I see them now.—That was all I wanted.

                                        [*Exit* THE GUARD
So that's all right.

ANATH.   Can you remember your cousin?

TEUSRET. Why, which cousin?

ANATH.   My foster son. You knew him
When you were little. He lived with us in the palace.

TEUSRET. The birds are back on the roof now.

ANATH.   Moses, Teusret.

TEUSRET. What, Aunt? Yes, I think I remember. I remember
A tall uncle. Was he only a cousin?
He used to drum his helmet with a dagger
While he sang us regimental marches to get us to sleep.
It never did. Why?

ANATH.   No reason. I thought of him.
Well, they've buried the man in the sand. We'd better
Find our morning again and use what's left.

TEUSRET. Why did you think of him? Why *then* particularly?

ANATH. Why not then? Sometimes he blows about my brain
Like litter at the end of a public holiday.
I have obstinate affections. Ask your father.
He would tell you, if it wasn't impolitic
To mention Moses, what a girl of fire
I was, before I made these embers.
He could tell you how I crossed your grandfather,
And your grandfather was a dynasty in himself.
Oh Teusret, what a day of legend that was!
I held forbidden Israel in my arms
And growled on my stubborn doorstep, till I had my way.

TEUSRET. What do you mean?

ANATH.   Well, never mind.

TEUSRET.
You've told me so far.

ANATH.   Keep it to yourself then.
The summer of '24 had brilliant days
And unprecedented storms. The striped linen
You once cut up for a doll's dress was the dress
Made for me that summer. It was the summer
When my father, your grandfather, published the pronounce-
ment.

TEUSRET. What pronouncement?

ANATH.   That all the boys of Jewdom
Should be killed. Not out of spite, Teusret; necessity.
Your grandfather ordered that Defence of the Realm be painted
At the head of the document, in azure and silver.
It made it easier for him.

TEUSRET.   Were they killed?

ANATH. Yes, they all died of a signature. Or we thought so,
Until the thirtieth of August. I went bathing on that day.
I was a girl then, Teusret, and played with the Nile
As though with a sister. And afterwards as I waded
To land again, pushing the river with my knees,
The wash rocked a little ark out
Into the daylight: and in the ark I found
A tiny weeping Israel who had failed
To be exterminated. When I stooped
With my hair dripping on to his face
He stopped in a screwed-up wail and looked.
And when I found my hands and crowded him
Into my breast, he buried like a burr.
And when I spoke I laughed, and when I laughed
I cried, he was so enchanting. I was ready
To raise a hornet's nest to keep him; in fact
I raised one. All the court flew up and buzzed.
But what could they do? Not even my Pharaoh-father
Could sting him out of my arms. So he grew up
Into your tall cousin, Egyptian
From beard to boots and, what was almost better,
A soldier of genius. You don't remember
How I held you on this terrace, to see him come home from war?
It was ten years ago. Do you remember

The shrieking music, and half Egypt shouting
Conqueror! Peacemaker!

TEUSRET. No.

ANATH. They have all tried to forget.
They have blotted him out of the records, but not out
Of my memory.

TEUSRET. Why did they blot him out?

ANATH. I might have known that I should say too much.

TEUSRET. Aunt, you must tell me.

ANATH. Well, no doubt I meant to.
The day I held you here, he came as the conqueror
Of Abyssinia. In all the windows and doors
Women elbowed and cracked their voices; and men
Hung on the gates and the trees; and children sang
The usual songs, conducted by their teachers.

TEUSRET. Yes, but what happened to make him——

ANATH. All right, I'm coming to it, Teusret. The day after,
For the country-side also to be able to see the hero,
He went to inspect the city being built at Pithom.—
My book was closed from that day forward.
He went round with an officer who unfortunately
Was zealous but unintelligent. Silly man:
Silly, silly man. He found a labourer
Idling or resting, and he thought, I suppose,
'I'll show this prince that I'm worth my position'
And beat the workman. A Jewish bricklayer.
He beat him senseless.

TEUSRET. And then?

ANATH. Moses turned—turned to what was going on—
Turned himself and his world turtle. It was
As though an inward knife scraped his eyes clean.

C

The General of Egypt, the Lion and the Prince
Recognized his mother's face in the battered body
Of a bricklayer; saw it was not the face above
His nursery, not my face after all.
He knew his seed. And where my voice had hung till then
Now voices descending from ancestral Abraham
Congregated on him. And he killed
His Egyptian self in the self of that Egyptian
And buried that self in the sand.

TEUSRET.   Aunt—

Enter A GUARD

GUARD.   The Pharaoh.
Madam, the Pharaoh is here.

ANATH.   Can we look innocent?

Enter SETI. *Exit* THE GUARD

TEUSRET. Good morning, father.

SETI.   Go indoors, my Teusret.

                                        [*Exit* TEUSRET

Where is Moses?

ANATH. Seti!

SETI.   Where is Moses? You will know.
In what country? Doing what?

ANATH.   Why Moses?

SETI. I need him.

ANATH.   I've no reason to remember.
I'm without him.

SETI.   But you know.

ANATH.   Why should I know?
   Why should I? When the sun goes down do I have to know
   Where and how it grovels under the world?
   I thought he was a dust-storm we had shut outside.
   Even now I sometimes bite on the grit.

SETI. I have found him necessary.
   Libya is armed along the length of her frontier,
   And the South's like sand, shifting and uncertain.
   I need Moses.—We have discarded in him
   A general of excellent perception.

ANATH. He's discarded, rightly or wrongly. We've let him go.

SETI. Deeds lie down at last, and so did his.
   Out in the wilderness, after two days' flight,
   His deed lay down, knowing what it had lost him.
   Under the boredom of thorn-trees he cried out
   For Egypt and his deed died. Ten years long
   He has lugged this dead thing after him.
   His loyalty needn't be questioned.

ANATH. We're coming to something strange when a normal day
   Opens and lets in the past. He may remember
   Egypt. He's in Midian.

SETI.   In what part of Midian?

ANATH. Wherever buckets are fetched up out of wells
   Or in his grave.

SETI.   We'll find him. If we have to comb
   Midian to its shadows we'll find him.

ANATH.   He's better where he is.

SETI. He is essential to my plans.

ANATH.   I tell you
He is better where he is. For you or me
He's better where he is.
We have seen different days without him
And I have done my hair a different way.
Leave him alone to bite his lips.

[SETI'S *eye is caught by something below and beyond the terrace*

SETI.   What's this,
What is this crowd?

ANATH.   It's Rameses! No qualms
For the dynasty, with a son as popular as he is.

SETI. There's half the city round him. Where are his guards?

ANATH. There: a little behind.

SETI.   The boy's too careless.
I'm not altogether at rest in the way he's growing,
His good graces for no-matter-whom.
He must learn to let the needs of Egypt rule him.

ANATH. He will learn. He is learning.

SETI.   Egypt should pray so.

ANATH. I would hazard a guess that Egypt's women
Have prayed for him often enough. Ra, raising
An eyebrow stiff with the concentration of creation
Probably says: That boy again? We'd better
Make something of him early and have them satisfied.
O, Rameses will be all right.

SETI.   I hope,
I hope.

                    Enter RAMESES, *a boy of eighteen*

RAMESES. Did you see the excitement? I think it's the drought.
Like the air, we're all quivering with heat.

Do you find that, Aunt? Either you must sleep like the dead
Or something violent must happen.

ANATH.   Look: your father.

RAMESES. I didn't see you, father. I'm sorry, sir.
Did I interrupt state matters?

SETI.   What morning have you had?

RAMESES. Holiday—books rolled up, military exercises
Over, and no social engagements. I've been fowling
Down at the marshes.

ANATH.   Any luck?

RAMESES.   Not much flesh
But a paradise of feathers. I was out before daybreak.

ANATH. It's a good marksman who hunts by batlight.

RAMESES.   But I
Waited for daylight. Until then the marsh was a torpor.
I clucked and clapped as the sun rose
And up shot so much whistle and whirr
I could only hold my spear and laugh.
All the indignant wings of the marshes
Flocking to the banner of Tuesday
To avoid the Prince of Egypt!
Off they flapped into the mist
Looking about for Monday
The day they had lived in peace: and finding nothing
Back they wheeled to Tuesday.
I had recovered myself by then and killed
One that had the breast of a chestnut.
At last he could feel the uninterrupted darkness
Of an addled egg. I watched his nerves flinching
As they felt how dark that darkness was.
I found myself trying to peer into his death.

It seemed a long way down. The morning and it
Were oddly separate,
Though the bird lay in the sun: separate somehow
Even from contemplation.

ANATH.   Excellent spirits
To make a success of a holiday.

RAMESES.   Only for a moment.

SETI. This afternoon I have business for you.   [*He turns to go in*

RAMESES.   Very well.

SETI. Was that thunder?

ANATH.   They're dumping new stone for the
                                                pyramid.

RAMESES. Two men came through the marshes before I left;
Jews, but not our Jews: or one of them
Was not; he seemed a man of authority
Although some miles of sun and dust were on him.

SETI. Aliens?

RAMESES.   Yes; but one of them I felt
I should have known. How could I?
I passed them again as I came home. They stood
To watch the crowd. I looked across and smiled
But got no smiles from them. And one, the tall one——

ANATH. Very tall?

RAMESES.   Yes, he was tall. It was he
Who is somehow in my memory.

ANATH.   Seti——

SETI.   Well?

ANATH. Is it possible that someone hasn't waited to be recalled?
Is it possible?

SETI.   It is not possible.

ANATH. Your thoughts are leaning that way too.
Sometimes the unaccountable stalks in.

SETI. Which way were they travelling, Rameses?

RAMESES. This way. If I had only thought of them sooner
We could have seen them go by.—Sir!
They are standing here at the foot of the stairway. How long
Can they have been there? Shall I speak to them?

ANATH. He has stood all day under my brain's stairway.
Seti, who is there? Which foremost, Rameses?
The tall one?

RAMESES.   Yes. Who's in your mind?

ANATH.   The tall one.
The tall one.

                     [RAMESES *goes down the steps*
        So he is back; and small-talk
Has to block a draught up ten years old.

SETI. Why has he come?

ANATH.   You said he longed for Egypt.

SETI. I think so.

ANATH.   But what am I in Egypt?
A dead king's daughter.

     Re-enter RAMESES, *followed by* MOSES *and* AARON

SETI.   What words can I find to fit
So ghostly a homecoming? Understand you are welcome.
Whatever uncertainty you have can go.
We welcome you. Look who is here.

ANATH. He has seen me. We have looked at one another.

SETI. We'll absolve ourselves of the ten years. Who is this?

MOSES. My brother.

SETI. I had not heard you had a brother.

ANATH. A brother, a sister—and a mother. All the three.

SETI. I told my sister we must have you back.
And so we must, and so Egypt must; and it seems
That we have. You are come promptly at the word, Moses.

MOSES. This is not why I came.

SETI. You would scarcely foresee it.

MOSES. I am not who you think. I am a stranger.

SETI. Not by a vein or a hair. The past is forgotten.
You are a prince of Egypt.

MOSES. The prince of Egypt
Died the day he fled.

SETI. What do you mean?

MOSES. That prince of Egypt died. I am the Hebrew
Smitten out of the shadow of that prince,
Vomited out of his dry lips, the cry
Whipped off the sanded tongue of that prince of Egypt.

SETI. What has this long discomfort done for you,
My friend? It has made you bitter.

MOSES. Why was it you decided to ask me to come back?

SETI. Isn't it time we laid the crippling ghost
That haunts us? You evidently thought so too
To come so far.

MOSES. You've a better reason than that.

SETI. Why should you want reasons when you have come
On your own initiative? Why are you here?
I am asking you candidly. Why did you come?

MOSES. My blood heard my blood weeping
Far off like the swimming of fear under the sea,
The sobbing at night below the garden. I heard
My blood weeping. It is here it wept and weeps.
It was from here I heard coming this drum of despair,
Under your shoes, under your smile, and under
The foundations of your tomb. From Egypt.

ANATH. What was it, Seti, that lay down and died?

SETI. Why are you here?

MOSES.   To be close to this that up to now
Has been a pain in the mind, not yet
Possessing the mind, but so increasing
It has driven me here, to be in myself the pain,
To be the pain's own life.

SETI.   Still you haven't
Answered my question. Come, what do you want?

MOSES. First, that you should know what you are doing.

SETI. Take care, Moses.

ANATH.   And secondly?

MOSES.   What can I hope
From that until he has understood the first?

SETI. What is this mood you have come in which is so ready
To abuse a decent welcome? There is something shipwreck
About you that will not do for peaceful places.
Steady yourself if we're to understand one another.
I am the Pharaoh, Moses, not the young uncle
Of the Heliopolis classroom, nor your messroom brother.

MOSES. A man has more to be than a Pharaoh.
  He must dare to outgrow the security
  Of partial blindness. I'm not speaking now
  To your crown; I'm speaking to your merciless mischief.

SETI. You have coarsened during your exile. What you say
  Hasn't even the virtue of clarity. If you wish
  To consider my offer of reinstatement, go
  And consider. I can be patient. Egypt can do
  Her work on you like a generous woman, given
  Her time.   [*He glances at* ANATH
      Midian will wash off in the Nile.
  Go on, go on, I shall not remember this morning.

MOSES. I think you will. My brother has lived these days
  In amongst Israel, while I was sleeping.
  He knows both the truth and the injury better than I can.
  Let him speak what he knows.

AARON. Twelve hundred thousand Israelites are under
  Your dominion. Of these two hundred and twenty thousand
  Only, are men. The rest are in the proportion
  Of four hundred and fifty thousand women
  And five hundred and thirty thousand children.

SETI. I have my census-takers.

AARON.   So perhaps
  Has Death got his; but I think he has not referred
  His undertakings to your dynastic understanding.
  Here I have his estimate: between April and July
  Six hundred and one deaths suffered in old age
  But an old age of forced labour, their backs bent twice,
  Under the weight of years and under the mule-whip.
  Also thirty-eight deaths of healthy men
  Who made some show of reluctance or momentary
  Impatience.

MOSES.   That was a good cure. They are now
Patient for all eternity.

AARON.   Also the deaths
Of a hundred pregnant women, forced to dig
Until they had become their own gravediggers.
Also the deaths of eighty-four children, twelve
Unofficial crucifixions . . .

SETI.   This is intolerable
Singsong! Am I to compose the epitaphs
For every individual grave of this trying summer?
I have my figures. I do not need yours.
I have put men to a purpose who otherwise
Would have had not the least meaning.

MOSES. Not the least meaning, except the meaning
Of the breath in your lungs, the mystery of existing
At all. What have we approached or conceived
When we have conquered and built a world? Even
Though civilization became perfect? What then?
We have only put a crown on the skeleton.
It is the individual man
In his individual freedom who can mature
With his warm spirit the unripe world.
They are your likeness, these men, even to nightmares.
I have business with Egypt, one more victory for her,
A better one than Ethiopia:
That she should come to see her own shame
And discover justice for my people.

SETI. You have fermented in your Midian bottle.
But lately I have learnt an obstinate patience.
We should have done better to have met
Out of the sun. We can do better than this
And so we shall yet, later, at a cooler time.

Where will you sleep? We will see you have food.
Do you remember, I wonder, the palace nectarine?
I said, where will you lodge?

MOSES.   With my sister, Miriam.

SETI [*to* ANATH]. Do you know where that is?

ANATH.   Perfectly.

SETI [*going in*].   Very well.

ANATH. Now he will not sleep again tonight.

MOSES. I hope that none of us will sleep again
Until we all can sleep.

ANATH.   And so once more
We see each other. You have chosen a fine day.

          [MOSES *waits.* ANATH *says no more. He goes with* AARON

ANATH. I taught him to walk, Rameses. I also taught him
To speak and say his alphabet. I taught you your
Alphabet also; and also Teusret hers.
I have been a really useful woman.

RAMESES.   Where
Does his sister live?

ANATH.   Why do you want to know?

RAMESES. I wondered where it might be.

ANATH.   She has a tent
By the brick-kiln.

RAMESES.   I liked that man.

ANATH. So have others before you. Like him, Rameses,
Forget him, and let us live in peace.

RAMESES. I shall go and find him.

ANATH. Rameses, I ask you to forget him.

RAMESES. How?

ANATH. What would make it difficult?

RAMESES. Can you forget him?

ANATH. He has gone.

RAMESES. And something of us, I think, went with him.

ANATH. Well, you will let him go. I have asked you.

RAMESES. No.
I love you, you know that. But trust me a little.
I shall be discreet. [*Exit* RAMESES

ANATH. Rameses!—No,
What should I be doing, turning his feet
Towards my fears? [*She goes to the parapet*
Enter TEUSRET

TEUSRET. Aunt Anath, where is Rameses going?
Aunt Anath—

ANATH. Do you remember, Teusret?
A man fell from the pyramid—only this morning.

CURTAIN

SCENE TWO

MIRIAM'S *tent.* MOSES [*in the entrance*]. MIRIAM.

MOSES. Miriam! Miriam!

MIRIAM. Is it my brother? Yes;
You have his immovable look. Aaron told me
To expect you.

MOSES. Can you be Miriam?

MIRIAM.   A kind
  Of residue. Sit down, if you don't mind.
  I dislike answering questions. Ask me nothing.
  I am very well; I have nothing to offer you
  To drink.

MOSES.   I'm glad to be with you after so long.

MIRIAM. You will find it very tiresome after five or six minutes.
  I repeat myself unendurably, like the Creation.
  Your only hope is to deaden yourself to me
  And it.

AARON [*in the entrance*]. Your name runs like fire, like an ostrich!
  You didn't wait to hear, but the sergeant at the gate
  Was full of it. He said the whole city
  Is pulsing with talk and argument about you:
  As soon as this; before you've even been seen!

MOSES. And what will this do for us?

AARON.   Surely it suggests
  They're taking sides? Down in the square, it seems, a minister's
      wife
  Was wearing an M in small lilies; her daughter snatched them off
  And threw them among the pigeons. How can Seti
  Assure himself what size your faction is?
  Egypt loves and hates you inextricably.

MOSES. Egypt is afraid. Love me? No;
  They're afraid to be without me.

AARON. That will pass for love.

MOSES. They love me from the bottom of their greed.
  Give me the bad news. What men have we lost?

MIRIAM. So you're not only here on a visit to your sister.

AARON. Here is a list. It's not complete.

MIRIAM.   I've had
Enough of trouble.

MOSES.   Rahnor, Janeth, Pathrusim—
Is he lost? Pathrusim? The sand of Egypt
Is abominably the richer.—Hadoram, Seth,
Havilah, Dodanim . . .

MIRIAM.   Why do you read
Dead men's names? There are some of us still breathing.
Your sister, for example, is still alive,
Figuratively speaking. I imagined
You would have plenty to tell me. Have you not?
Am I always to know nothing of you?

MOSES.   These names are what I am.

MIRIAM. They are yesterday's life. I liked many of them very well;
But we no longer have anything in common.

AARON. Are we to forget them because we have lost them?

MIRIAM.   To wish
To be with them comes too easily.

MOSES.   This tent
Is stifling.

MIRIAM.   I keep it closed. I have no liking
For what goes on outside.

MOSES.   When do they say
The mountains last had rain?

MIRIAM.   Nine months ago.

MOSES. It's time for parturition.
Look: what you shut out is a withering city.
City of Egypt. This land once I worshipped,
And now I cannot be sure what I bring against her
In my heart. This noon, like every other noon,

Still groans with the laborious wheels which drew
The Nile water. There is little difference
Between ourselves and those blindfolded oxen.
We also do the thing we cannot see,
Hearing the creaking pivot and only knowing
That we labour.

MIRIAM.   Why did you bring him? Take yourselves off!
This is my tent, and it's not for restless hands.
He's a dangermaker still.

AARON. What has he said, Miriam?

MIRIAM.   I have a son
And that is all I rest on. There's a man
Who should have been my brother. A king's daughter
Swallowed him and spat out this outlaw. I'll
Not have any more in the family.

AARON.   What should make them?

MIRIAM. You and he. I know. Two years ago
I had it all: the surly men coming in here,
One at a time by signal, hardly nodding
Towards me, covering the table with their knife-cuts
To show how revolution must come, and freedom,
And idiocy; till a beetle striking the lamp
Or the coal settling, would shiver through us all
As though a dagger had sung into the pole.
And Espah and Zoad are dead from it. And you
In a night of loud hyenas went over the border.
Not again. I'll keep my nights of sleep, and I'll keep
My son.

AARON.   In this country of murder?

MIRIAM.   I'll keep my son
In whatever country.

MOSES. Happily?

MIRIAM. We have
A way of living. We have the habit. Well?
It becomes a kind of pleasantness.

MOSES. You have gone
With the dead after all, but you pretend not to see them.
Miriam, we have to speak to them with our lives.
Death was their question to us, and our lives
Become their understanding or perplexity.
And by living to answer them, we also answer
Our own impermanence. But this rule of Egypt
Denies us life, Miriam, and gives us nothing
With which we can outspeak our graves.

MIRIAM. I am angry;
The pity is I am angry. I must pretend
You have said nothing.

AARON. But do you understand him?
In fact, do I understand him?

MOSES. When I was a child,
Miriam, and you would come to me in the huge
Nursery of the Pharaohs, we'd go hand
In hand along your stories, Hebrew stories
Which like contraband you put quietly in
To become my nature. Do you remember?

MIRIAM. How she disliked me then! But what a talent
For condescension she had. I never saw you
After you were a child except by waiting
Among the crowd in the streets. There was no need
To come from Midian to tell me what my life is;
I have a bowing acquaintance with it. I knew it
When I hid you to save you from the knives.

Before I could talk it talked to me
In most difficult words.

MOSES.   What words, Miriam?

MIRIAM. Pogrom, for one. And the curses of Egyptian children
When I ran towards them expecting to play;
The shout of command kicking at the ribs,
All human words torn to a scream.
We have a wildfowl quality of blood,
Moses, temptation for sportsmen.

MOSES.   Go on.

MIRIAM.   With what,
If you please? Do you know the secret which will change
Our spoor? Our grandfather was stoned. I imagine
Creation tried our blood, and brought it in guilty.

MOSES. It was the verdict of Chaos.

MIRIAM.   Let us alone
To serve the sentence. One grows accustomed.
We have to be as we are.

MOSES.   We have
To be Israel; as we are.

MIRIAM. Where do you see Israel now?

MOSES.   Where
Do I see God? Be certain, Israel is.
I am here to be a stone in her sling, out of her gall.

MIRIAM. Israel! Israel's the legend I told you in the nursery.
We've no more spirit to support a God.

MOSES. We have a God who will support the spirit,
And both shall be found. But still I need to know how good
Can be strong enough to break out of the possessing

Arms of evil. I am there, beyond myself,
If I could reach to where I am.

AARON.   You will find the approach
And the means you want, I'm confident. Something
Will soon open a way to action.

RAMESES [*in the tent opening*].   Uncle.
I knew you as that. When I have thought of you
It has been as my uncle. You may not like it.
You may not want to see me, even.

MOSES. Welcome and unwelcome.

RAMESES.   I haven't come
From my father. I used schoolboy's worship, like myrrh
And cassia, to perpetuate you:
The immense and affable god in general's uniform,
Who came and went between wars, who filled the schoolroom;
And I could call him uncle. So when the memory
Broke its wrappings, and stood speaking like a man
On a noonday terrace, I decided to come nearer.

MOSES. Come on, then, and send the god to vanish finally
Into the lie that he always was.

RAMESES.   You spoke
To my father too suddenly.

MOSES.   Yes, we're precipitous,
We gods. We threw off the world, vegetable
And animal too, on the impulse of an imaginative
Moment. But we lost interest.

RAMESES.   You mean
I'm a boy to you still.

MOSES.   You came by your boyhood honestly.
Mine I stole. I had no right to it.

AARON.   Why
Do you turn him away, Moses? Why not talk to him?

MOSES. What would we talk of, Aaron? What quiet subject?
They tell me centuries of horror brood
In this vivid kingdom of fertile mud. Do you think
If we swung the rattle of conversation
Those centuries would fly off like so many crows?
They would wheel above us and come to feed again.

AARON. But where shall we find a better
Opportunity?

RAMESES.   I have my father mapped
So that I know which way to travel. Listen,
Uncle—he says he would have recalled you, which means
He needs you here. He'll be friendly if you let him.
I kept a buckle of your uniform—this one, the lion-head.
Take it again, take our army and be our general.
You'll become inseparable from Egypt's safety;
Then he will listen. Then you can direct
His goodwill past yourself to these Israelites.

AARON. It's true. You have the buckle, and we're agreed, then.
My dreams were less; not a third as felicitous.

MOSES. Egypt and Israel both in me together!
How would that be managed? I should wolf
Myself to keep myself nourished. I could play
With wars, oh God, very pleasantly. You know
I prosper in a cloud of dust—you're wise
To offer me that. And Egypt would still be,
In spite of my fathers, a sufficient cause.

AARON. Yes, it would be sufficient.

MOSES.   Splendid, then.
What armour shall I wear? What ancestral metal
Above my heart? Rib, thighbone and skull:
Bones from the mines of Egypt. I will clank
To Egypt's victory in Israel's bones.
Does this please you? Does it not? Admire
How when preparing a campaign I become
Oblivious to day and night, and in
The action, obsessed. How will that do? I make
My future, put glory into Egypt, enjoy myself
Into your father's confidence—yes, that,
I know; and being there, perhaps I coax
Little concessions for the Hebrew cause
To justify me.—Idiot, idiot!
I should have lost them, Aaron, and be lost,
More than when in Midian I sat
Over my food and let them trudge in my bowels.

AARON. I have faith in your judgement. Nevertheless, this is
Something to be thought of, a reality of a kind.

MOSES. Like adultery.

MIRIAM.   Offer of a generalship?
Of course I don't understand. But like adultery?
To be a general? Do you mean us to think
You would refuse—

MOSES.   You both would like to see
Your brother fat, but your brother has a fancy
To be as lean as Israel.

RAMESES.   Will you promise to be patient?
There will be difficulties to be got over;
I have a father. But at some future time
When I am Pharaoh—

MOSES.   By then I may be free
To let my bones talk of their disinterest
In the world's affairs: and whether it is Hebrew
Or Egyptian, man will cry for me no longer.

MIRIAM. Listen!

AARON.   What is it?

MIRIAM.   Nothing, nothing—I imagined—
Why should he be back at this time? What
Could bring him now? Listen!

MOSES.   What do you hear?

MIRIAM. It's the call he gives when he's reaching home.

AARON.   Her son.
It's Shendi.

MIRIAM.   Something has happened.
Why is the palace here? What are you doing here
In my home? He cannot even come home.

RAMESES.   Is this
Egypt?

MIRIAM. Do you hear him again? No nearer, no nearer.
He is being prevented. Can I get to him
Without being seen? Stay where you are. No one
Must see me, no one.
                    [*She goes out. In a moment* AARON *follows her*

RAMESES.   You all think of me
As an enemy.

MOSES.   We're not enemies so much
As creatures of division. You and I,
Rameses, like money in a purse,
Ring together only to be spent
For different reasons.

There will be summers to come
Which need the throne and lotus: a world
Richer for an Egypt prosperous in wisdom
Which you will govern.

RAMESES.   Am I never to see you?

MOSES. No, it would be better, never. Stay with your own:
A people without blame which still
Faces the good future. My own purpose
Would only bring you confusion. Forget me, Rameses.

RAMESES. That anyway is impossible. I know
I bear your mark, and how will you obliterate
That? Do you forget the feel of the year
When you were as I am? They count me as a man,
Just. But the boy is still in my head and mouth.
I feel him there. I speak him. I should burn
Throne and lotus gladly if I could break
Myself of boyhood, if burning would do it. But you
Are clear and risen roundly over the hazes.
You have the formula. I need it.

MOSES.   Clear?
Evidence of that! Where in this drouthy
Overwatered world can you find me clarity?
What spirit made the hawk? a bird obedient
To grace, a bright lash on the cheek of the wind
And drawn and ringed with feathered earth and sun,
An achievement of eternity's birdsmith. But did he
Also bleak the glittering charcoal of the eyes
And sharpen beak and claws on his hone of lust?
What language is life? Not one I know.
A quarrel in God's nature. But you, at least,
Are pronounceable: heir of Egypt, heir of Egypt.
That is yourself.

RAMESES.   You mean I'm of no value
Except to be Egypt's ornament.

MOSES.   Of much
Value; infinite.

RAMESES.   But we stay unfriendly?

MOSES. Because I taste your boyhood and remember mine
And like them both.

RAMESES.   But even so—

MOSES.   You shall stay as you are.

RAMESES. Exactly as I am, a friend of Moses.

MOSES. They're coming with Shendi. Keep with me in the shadow.

Enter MIRIAM *and* AARON, *supporting* SHENDI

MIRIAM. He has been so strong. Are you ill? How are you ill?
You can speak, surely you can speak? We don't know them;
That's what is worst—our own—even in childhood
They say so little.

AARON.   Lie here, Shendi.

MIRIAM.   Still
And quiet. What shall I do for him?

AARON.   Give him this water.

MIRIAM. A sip, and then you shall have more.

SHENDI. They'll come.

MIRIAM.   Keep yourself quiet.

SHENDI.   Yes, they will come,
They'll come for me, they'll find me!

AARON.   What have you done?

MIRIAM. Done?

SHENDI.   What are you holding me for? Must I always
Be held? It was the sun! Don't you know that?
They make madmen in the sun. Thousands of madmen
Have been made in the sun. They say nothing, nothing at all,
But suddenly they're running—no, not they,
It's only their bodies that are running: the madmen
Are still standing in the sun, watching their bodies
Run away. Can they kill me for that? Or what, or what?
It was the strike that started it!

AARON.   What have you said!
What strike?

MIRIAM.   He's ill!

SHENDI.   No, it was the sun; not the strike,
The sun. The noise of the strike, the whips.

AARON.   The strike?
What was it? What do you mean?

SHENDI.   The spermy bastards!
They make us hit the earth like spit.

MIRIAM.   What are you saying?
Don't ask him any more!

AARON.   I'll make him tell me. What strike?
What are you saying?

SHENDI.   I don't know what has happened.
The brickmakers began it. A youngster was with me,
Twelve years old, and he left me to watch the trouble.
I saw them take him away, they dragged him off
To the captain at the gate, because he was watching.
It has nothing to do with it. It's the sun. Have you heard
The order? They'll not give us straw to make the bricks;
We must gather the straw ourselves; but the tale of bricks

Must be more, more! What does it matter? Who says
It matters? They're coming for me.

MIRIAM.   It cannot happen,
Shendi, it cannot.

MOSES.   Cannot happen, cannot be.
Cannot. Earth, life, ourselves are impossibility;
What is this Pharaoh who answers me with this?

SHENDI.   Who's that?
My uncle, is it? The great fellow that was.
The man who thought he was Egypt. Have you come
To try again, murderer? Look at your crop of relations
And how they do in the land you dunged for us.
Do you hear that? They're whipping the side of the tent.
You know I can't stand up, they've come for me,
You know it was the sun—uncle, uncle!

MIRIAM. It was neighbours talking, it was only the neighbours.
                                                —Aaron,
It was neighbours talking. Wasn't it, wasn't it?

                    Enter TWO OVERSEERS

                                              No, no!

1ST OVERSEER. Nice family. Here's the man we want.

2ND OVERSEER.   Get up,
Little rat. So you'd strike? We'll teach you striking.
Striking's our speciality. Eh? Not bad! We'll strike him!

MIRIAM. He's sick—can't you see?

1ST OVERSEER.   That's enough of that.

RAMESES.   What is this?
Weren't you told I had sent for him?

2ND OVERSEER.   My crimes!

RAMESES. Well, weren't you told?

1ST OVERSEER.　　　　　No, sir; no, your holiness; not told.
I beg your pardon, sir. I didn't see you, my lord, didn't see you.

RAMESES. I tell you now. I sent for him. Go away.

1ST OVERSEER. Yes, lord.

2ND OVERSEER.　　　　Yes, almighty.
　　　　　　　　　　　[*They back away out of sight*

MIRIAM. You're here, Shendi, you're here. The prince has kept
　you.
　He spoke for you.

SHENDI. No one warned—What are you doing with me?
　Is it a trick? What did I say before they came?
　My lord forgive me, I was ill.

RAMESES. Nothing will hurt you. You can rest.
　You have seen enough of Egypt in this tent.
　　　　　　　　　　　　　　　[*Exit* RAMESES

AARON. I begin to have hope.
　Eh, Moses? This is the boy who will be our man,
　The palace key. In the belly of our misfortune
　We find our hope.

MOSES.　　　　　We're not concerned with hope,
　Or with despair; our need is something different:
　To confront ourselves, to create within ourselves
　Existence which cannot fail to be fulfilled.
　It will not be through this boy, nor through
　Thankless palace manœuvring and compromise.

AARON. Where will you turn, then?

MOSES.　　　　　　Where shall I look for triumph?
　Somewhere, not beyond our scope, is a power
　Participating but unharnessed, waiting
　To be led towards us. Good has a singular strength

Not known to evil; and I, an ambitious heart
Needing interpretation. But not through Rameses,
Never through Rameses. I will not use him!

CURTAIN

SCENE THREE

A room in the Palace, giving on to the terrace of Scene One. ANATH *is
standing on the terrace.* TEUSRET'S *voice is heard calling 'Rameses!
Rameses!' It draws nearer.* ANATH *comes into the room and listens
for* TEUSRET'S *voice which now comes from farther away. She turns
to go back to the terrace. Enter* RAMESES.

ANATH. Have you seen your father?

RAMESES. He has made me a present of my future
With the royal seal attached. I'm to marry
The King of Syria's daughter. Did you know?

ANATH. He told me he would ask this of you.

RAMESES. When I woke this morning I thought nothing of the
    future,
Only of today, and what I remembered of the past.
And yet in these twelve hours the future
Has suddenly come up, two-legged, huge, as though to say
'See nothing but me.' First Moses, with his fixed purpose
Walking ahead of us, as absolute
As a man's death. And now this other future,
A stranger from Syria to be the focus
Of my life, my senses and devotion, if it may be.

ANATH. I wish you happiness.

RAMESES.   Where is Teusret?

ANATH. Everywhere.
Put your hand in one place, she is already
Beating her wings in another.

RAMESES. Listen—look—
What is this 'now', the moment we're now crossing?
Can this truth vanish?
Look, your shadow thrown over the chair,
That dog's jerking bark, the distance of whistling,
A gate clanging-to, the water thrown into the yard,
Your fingers travelling your bracelet, my voice—listen,
My voice—your breathing—

[TEUSRET *is heard calling* RAMESES

And Teusret running through the empty rooms.
It is true for us now, but not till now, and never
To be again. I want it for myself.
This is my life.

Enter TEUSRET

It has gone.

TEUSRET. I've found you at last.
Where have you been hidden? Where were you?

RAMESES. With father.

TEUSRET. For an hour!
No one could tell me. The rooms were all deserted.
Just as it happens in my sleep sometimes; but then
The door on the other side of the room is always
Closing behind you, and the room is empty—I never
Come to you.

RAMESES. But, awake, it's different. You find me.

TEUSRET. Why did he talk for so long?

RAMESES.   I'm to be married
  He says.

TEUSRET. I had a riddle to ask you. Fareti
  Taught it to me.

RAMESES.   What is it?

TEUSRET.   Rameses,
  When will you be married?

RAMESES.   Soon, he says.

TEUSRET. Why? Why? You can't! What does he mean?
  Then—if you did—Why have you said so? Oh,
  Why did you say it?

RAMESES.   Teusret—

TEUSRET.   Who is it?

RAMESES.   The Syrian.
  Her name is Phipa.

TEUSRET.   Do you think that's pretty?
  Phipa, Phipa, Phipa! The noise a flute makes
  When the mouth's too full of saliva. You won't do it.

RAMESES. What can I say?

ANATH.   Teusret, we all, you will find,
  Belong to Egypt: our lives go on the loom
  And our land weaves. And the gods know we need
  Some such alliance. If the dynasty is safe
  We can at least be partly ourselves. He will need
  Both of us still.

TEUSRET.   He won't. He will be changed.
  The days will be different and I shall be the same.
  How shall I be happy then?

                    Enter SETI

                                        Will *you* be?
Are you glad?

SETI.   Can you imagine, Teusret,
  The frantic compulsion which first fetched man forming
  And breathing out of the earth's dust? Such
  A compulsion of beauty has this Phipa of Syria,
  With the addition of wit and a good head for business.
  She's immensely rich. Homegoing sailors,
  When there are no stars, steer perfectly for Syria
  Merely by thinking of her. So they say.
  A figure of her, hung under the stern
  And kissing the wake, ensures a harvest of fish.

TEUSRET. What a tale!

SETI.   Well, yes, but she has beauty.

TEUSRET.   Flowers for Rameses
  Then! We must make it an occasion. I'll fetch my lute
  And celebrate. Garlands! I'll make you into
  A nice little afternoon god. Don't go away.

RAMESES. Here, Teusret—

TEUSRET.   You have earned a ceremony.
  Would you rather have me in tears? This isn't silliness
  But a proper formality. I need to do it.
  Wait, all of you.   [*Exit* TEUSRET

ANATH.   Let her do what she must.

RAMESES.   Father,
  I have something to ask you. It has to do with Moses.

SETI. He needn't trouble you.

RAMESES.   Nor any of us. But haven't you
  Overlooked his nephew?

SETI.   This is nothing to you.
  Nothing to you at all.

RAMESES.   Nothing at all.
  Moses has a sister and a nephew.
  The nephew's a labourer. Might there not here be a way
  By which you could come at Moses?

SETI.   Statesmanship,
  My son, is the gods' gift to restrain their own
  Infidelities to man. As for Moses,
  I'll comprehend him when he's comprehensible.

RAMESES. Such as a commission for this nephew; or a place in the
      palace.
  What do you say? Can you talk of honours
  To a man whose family is unhonoured? I don't know,
  But you will know.

SETI.   Who told you to speak of him?
  What do you know of this name that you're bandying? Anath?
  Is this your influence?

ANATH.   Am I a planet,
  To be so influential? No, Seti, it is not.
  I would rather infect him with something less dubious
  Than the blood of Moses.

                        Enter TEUSRET *with a lute and flowers*

TEUSRET.   Look, I have them. I got them
  Out of my room. They were round my bronze Isis.
  Shall I have offended her?

SETI.   Do you know this nephew?

ANATH. I've seen him.

SETI.   How did he promise?

ANATH.   He promised to be male,
As though he might have the ability for a beard
I thought.

TEUSRET. Are you all ready for the ceremony?
Rameses, you must be in a chair; this chair.

RAMESES. Can it be tried?

SETI.   What is it now?

RAMESES.   To mark
My coming of age. May I commission the nephew?

SETI. That is still to be known. I must have precise
Information of him. Now forget the question.

TEUSRET. Why must you go
Before you see Rameses in flowers? And when
Have you ever heard me play on my lute?   [*Exit* SETI
                              Has no one
Told him he has a daughter?

ANATH.   The flowers were schooled
With salamanders, to be so enduring
In this furnace.

RAMESES.   Will he really do it?

ANATH.   The land
Is rocking, remember. He'll take hold even of grass.

TEUSRET. Let me begin. Neither of you has any sense
Of occasion. These on your shoulders. What *are* flowers?
What is the bridge to be crossed, I wonder,
From a petal to being a wing or a hand? These
For your brows. Does the scent of them sicken you?
My pollen fingers.

RAMESES.   They're shattering already.

                                        D

TEUSRET. Some of them are too full.

RAMESES.   You've brought me the garden.
  Here's an earwig on my hand.

TEUSRET.   Tread on it. Now
  You're ripe to receive a god. Isn't he, Aunt?
  Does he look noble? My brother in bloom.

RAMESES [*treading on the earwig*]. Out goes he. Let's get your singing over.

TEUSRET [*staring*]. I have to remember you. Sing with me.

ANATH.   I?
  Sing? With the crack in my voice? Not songs for bridegrooms.
  Only songs in the minor, where a false note
  Can be taken to be excessive sensibility.

TEUSRET. Nothing, nothing will go on in the old way.
  I wonder, can I remember which is the key? [*She touches the lute*

RAMESES. Did you know my father had ordered the Israelites
  To gather their own straw?

ANATH.   Yes, I knew.

RAMESES.   Why did he?

ANATH. A little show of invulnerability.

RAMESES. Is Moses safe here?

TEUSRET.   I wish there were echoes in this room,
  A choir of them, to be company for my voice.
  You will have to help me when I lose myself.
  [*Sings*]   Why should there be two
                      Where one will do,
                  Step over this shadow and tell me
                  And my heart will make a ring
                      Sighing in a circle

And my hands will beckon and bring
The maiden fortune who befell me
O fortune, fortune.

Enter SETI

You see, father,—doesn't he look married already?
[*Sings*]   Why do we breathe and wait
So separate?
The whirl in the shell and the sand
Is time going home to time
Kissing to a darkness.
So shall we go, so shall we seem
In the gardens, hand in hand.
O fortune, fortune.
So changed against the sun—

[*She is interrupted by* MOSES, *who enters bearing in his arms
a dead Israelite boy*

ANATH. What are we to have now?

SETI. What is this? Isn't it enough that you broke
Into Egypt unasked but you must—

MOSES.   This is your property.
Of little value. Shall I bury it in your garden?
You need have no anxiety. It will not grow.

ANATH. Oh, in the name of the gods—

SETI.   Is your reason gone?

MOSES [*laying the body at* SETI'S *feet*]. Look: worthless, worthless.
The music needn't stop.
You killed him.

SETI.   As I thought; you've let your brain
Suffer in this heat. I saw, in the first few words
You spoke this morning, it would end in this.

TEUSRET. Rameses! That boy!

RAMESES.   That isn't death
  Lying on the ground.

TEUSRET.   It is! It is! It is!

SETI. Well? Tell me: is it an act of sanity
  To carry this child here? I'm sorry to see it.
  Take him and have him buried. You know it wasn't
  Done by me.

MOSES.   It was done of you. You'll not
  Escape from yourself through the narrows between By and Of.
  Your captain killed him on the metal of your gates, as with
  A score of others. If it wasn't done of you
  Fetch the captain, condemn him to death, and watch
  How he'll stare.

SETI.   I'll see the man. It 's understood.

MOSES. Who understands? And what is understood?
  If you move your foot only a little forward
  Your toe will be against your power. Is this
  How you imagined your strength to be—ungrowing,
  Unbreathing, a child, and dead? Out of him
  Comes your army, your fleet, the cliff of gold
  You move on, pride, place, adulation
  And name. Fetch in your captain,
  Fetch in your thousand captains, and condemn them
  For the murder of your power.

SETI.   Nature is lavish,
  And in return for being understood,
  Not hoarded, gives us civilization.
  Would you have the earth never see purple
  Because the murex dies? Blame, dear Moses,

The gods for their creative plan which is
Not to count the cost but enormously
To bring about.

MOSES.   And so they bring about
The enormity of Egypt. Is that the full
Ambition of your gods? Egypt is only
One golden eruption of time, one flying spark
Attempting the ultimate fire. But who can say
What secrets my race has, what unworked seams
Of consciousness in mind and soul? Deny
Life to itself and life will harness and ride you
To its purpose. My people shall become themselves,
By reason of their own god who speaks within them.
What I ask is that I may lead them peaceably
Into the wilderness for a space, to find
Their god and so become living men at last.

SETI. More favours, something new. What god is this?

MOSES. The inimitable patience who doesn't yet
Strike you down.

SETI.   He and I have something in common
If he has patience. My trust is Egypt
And the maturity of the world.

MOSES. You know well enough invasion is probable,
Unrest is in and out of doors, your southern half
Splits from the north, the lords at your table
Are looking down at their hands. And flowing through all
Is the misery of my blood. Let that be clean
First, and then your flesh may heal.

SETI.   Enough,
I have nursed you enough. Now dungeons can nurse you.
Your god can find you behind the walls
And return your reason when he will.

ANATH. Seti! Are you sure? Will the surly half
Of Egypt believe he was mad?

SETI.   Do you still play
At being his mother?

ANATH.   Do you think I do?

RAMESES. There could have been some other way than this.
Is only Israel present to you,
As once it was only Egypt?
Are you still Moses? Or who? Who are you?

ANATH. Does he know?

SETI.   A man without laws.

MOSES. What are the laws? Tell me, you taker of lives!
I am here by fury and the heart. Is that not
A law? I am here to appease the unconsummated
Resourceless dead, to join life to the living.
Is that not underwritten by nature? Is that
Not a law? Do not ask me why I do it!
I live. I do this thing. I was born this action.
Despite you, through you, upon you,
I am compelled.

    [*A distant long cracking sound of thunder.* MOSES *jerks back
his head to listen*

               Are we overheard? Behind
The door that shuts us into life, there is
An ear. Am I given the power
To do what I am?
What says the infinite eavesdropper?

      [*From horizon to horizon the sky is beaten into thunder*

CURTAIN TO ACT ONE

ACT TWO

SCENE ONE

MIRIAM'S *tent, the evening of the same day.* MOSES. AARON.

MOSES.   Look: I shall divide them
Into groups a hundred or a hundred and fifty strong,
Each with a man to lead them, one they can trust,
Such as this man you mention, Morshad—
And the man I spoke with this evening. Put them down.

AARON. Morshad and Zedeth. Yes, I have them.

MOSES.   And then
This morning's rioting, the man who started that,
Whatever his name is. Will they listen to him again?

                    [AARON *goes to the tent-opening and looks out*

He made his move too early, some few days
Too soon.

AARON.   I thought I felt the earth quiver.

MOSES. What is he called?

AARON.   The earth has moved. It stirred
Like an animal. Moses!

MOSES.   The man has a name. Put him down.

AARON. Something unnatural has come awake
Which should have slept until time was finished.
Listen! Did you hear a roar? A building
Has collapsed. The dust is like a cloud, higher
Than the city. Will you see?

(97)

MOSES.   We have something more to do
Than to listen to falling cities. The dust will settle
While we Hebrews die. Come on; give me the names.

AARON. Why does this mean nothing to you?
Why won't you come and see it?

MOSES.   The names, the names.

                        [MIRIAM *stands in the opening, with a pitcher*

MIRIAM. All the water is blood.

AARON.   Miriam! What is happening to the city?

MIRIAM. There's no water, no water. Nothing but blood.

AARON. Then my fear has foundation. The sun has set
On truth altogether. The evening's a perjury!
Let none of us be duped by it.

MIRIAM.   The water
Is blood. The river floods it over the fields.
The wells stink of it.

AARON.   What are you saying?

MIRIAM.   Go out then
And see it yourself. The men who were thirsty enough
To drink what came, are lying at the well-heads
Vomiting.

MOSES.   What men? Ours?

MIRIAM.   Egyptians.

MOSES.   Miriam,
What have you there?

MIRIAM.   I filled my pitcher. We all
Filled our pitchers, everyone, in spite of—

Do you think it could happen to us? To them
Perhaps, something might happen; to the others but not
To ourselves.

MOSES [*bringing his hand out of the pitcher*]. Not to ourselves. To
the others.

MIRIAM.   Your hand
Has water on it! It is water!

MOSES.   From which well
Was this drawn?

MIRIAM.   Our own. Are we likely to use the Egyptians'?
But I saw it, we all saw it.

MOSES.   The sun this last hour
Has been that colour. Doesn't it at evening
Fall directly on our well?

MIRIAM.   The sun? Are we
Talking about the sun? Tell me I'm lying
And look at my feet. We slopped in blood flooding
From the Nile. I saw the Egyptians who drank it.

MOSES.   The Nile.
The Egyptians! But this water came from our well
Not theirs.—Was I waiting, Aaron? I was waiting
Without expectation. But surely, I already knew?
We with our five bare fingers
Have caused the strings of God to sound.
Creation's mutehead is dissolving, Aaron.
Our lives are being lived into our lives.
We are known!

MIRIAM.   Do you think it was you who made the Egyptians
Vomit? We may as well all be mad.
Where is Shendi?

AARON.   What 's this?
  Isn't there confusion enough? Confusion I call it!
  A contradiction of what we have always known
  To be conclusive: an ugly and impossible
  Mistake in nature. And you, you of all men
  Accept it, identify yourself with it. It must be
  Denied. What has become of you since yesterday?
  Is it not possible still to be plain men
  Dealing with a plain situation? Must we see
  Visions? You were an unchallengeable leader once.
  That is the man I follow. A plain soldier.

MIRIAM. Where can Shendi be?

MOSES. The plainest soldier is sworn to the service of riddles.
  Our strategy is written on strange eternal paper.
  We may decide to advance this way or that way
  But we are lifted forward by a wind
  And when it drops we see no more of the world.
  Shall we live in mystery and yet
  Conduct ourselves as though everything were known?
  If, in battle upon the sea, we fought
  As though on land, we should be more embroiled
  With water than the enemy. Are we on sea
  Or land, would you say?

AARON.   Sea? Land? For pity's sake
  Stay with reality.

MOSES.   If I can penetrate
  So far.

MIRIAM. Why hasn't Shendi come home yet? It 's past his time.
  He should have stayed here the rest of the day.
  Will you let me out of this intolerable night?
  Are we going to stand here for ever?

SHENDI [*in the tent-opening*].　　　　Mother!

MIRIAM.　　　　　　　　　　　　Shendi,
Has nothing happened to you? Let me see you and be
Reassured. Were you harmed by what I saw?

SHENDI. What have you seen? Nothing happened? Everything!
We've stepped across to a new life. Where were we living?
It was the appearance, of course, the appearance of hell.
Nothing like it at all, except in our minds, our poor
Minds. I was going to make you try to guess,
But such an idea could never come at a guess.
They've made me an officer!

MIRIAM. I don't—understand what you mean.

SHENDI.　　　　　　　　　　　Your son! You see?
They've made him an officer. Like an Egyptian officer.
Like? I am one. We didn't know, that was all,
The world is perfectly fair, something to laugh at.
The ridiculous difference between me this morning
And now! They found I was better with head than hands.

MIRIAM. Shendi, did you come by way of the wells? Did you see
them?

SHENDI. I expect so. They say they're diseased. Can you imagine
How I felt when they took me by the arm and led me
Apart from the other men? I almost fought them.
I knew I was going to be beaten—

MIRIAM.　　　　　　　　　　　Shendi, stop!
What are you saying?

SHENDI.　　　　　　Hell is done, done,
Done with, over!

MOSES.　　　For you.

MIRIAM.   They would never do it.
But then tonight everything is to be believed.
Nothing has any truth and anything is true.

SHENDI. I report at the officers' quarters
In half an hour. I'll take some of my things
Along with me now. Has the world always been known
To spring such wonders, do you think? You're to live with me,
Mother, do you understand? Follow on later
And ask for the new officer. At the officers' quarters.
Have you something you can give me to wrap this linen in?
The Libyans have broken across the border and massacred
Two companies of the border regiment.

AARON.   What?
A massacre? When was this?

SHENDI.   I don't know when.
Where have you put my razor? Four hundred Egyptians
Killed, they say. They talked as though
I were already one of themselves. They say
There's also a rumour of revolution in the south.

AARON. Moses, do you hear?

SHENDI.   Where is my razor?

MIRIAM.   There.
Did you see the wells? I don't know what life's doing.
I don't know how we're to think.

AARON.   Ambitiously.
These incidents all march our way. The Libyans
Over the border—revolution—Time
Is preparing for us with a timely unrest.
We came to Egypt at the perfect hour as it happens.

SHENDI. That's enough of talk like that!

MIRIAM.　　　　　　　　　　　As it happens;
　　If we knew what happens. Shendi an officer!
　　Will this be what we want, at last? As the Nile
　　Happens into blood. Shendi an officer.

SHENDI. And the officers' quarters, remember: comfort.

MIRIAM.　　　　　　　　　　　　　　As massacre
　　And revolution happens. As tomorrow
　　Happens, whatever happens tomorrow.

SHENDI.　　　　　　　　　　Come on,
　　I must go.

MOSES.　　Refuse this commission.

SHENDI.　　　　　　　　　　What did you say?

MOSES. Refuse this commission.

MIRIAM.　　　　　　　Refuse it?

SHENDI.　　　　　　　　　　　Listen to that!
　　As my uncle happens, this is no surprise.
　　Only one of the family must rise
　　And glow in Egypt. The rest of us can keep
　　Against the ground, and lose the whole damned world
　　Because Moses prefers it. But in spite of that,
　　In spite of that, generous brother of my mother,
　　We hope to live a little.

AARON.　　　　　　　As who does not?
　　The Pharaoh, I quite see, will have his motives.
　　But we can outmove motives to our advantage;
　　And here surely is a kind of proffered hand.

MIRIAM. Why should he refuse? How could he refuse?

SHENDI.　　　　　　　　　　　　It's clear
　　Why he says it. It was he who came back for recognition
　　And I have got it.

MOSES.   Make yourself live, then, Shendi;
But be sure it is life. The golden bear Success
Hugs a man close to its heart; and breaks his bones.
What have they said, these Egyptians?
Come with us and we'll treat you well.
Not, come with us and we will treat
You and your people well.

AARON.   They will come in time
Even to say that.

SHENDI [*to* MOSES]. This sounds well
Indeed, from you!

MIRIAM.   Shendi is to be all
That he can become—all; and I say so,
I who made him. Am I to go on holding
The guilt for his unhappiness when opportunity
Offers to deliver me from it? Guilt it was,
And damnation, for giving him birth. This will let me loose!

SHENDI. Why do we listen to him? I know how to value
The first fairness I've known. If you think so little
Of being alive, uncle, you will find they're assembling
Spears to flash on Libya. Why not make something
Of that? The tradition is that, once upon a time,
You didn't know the meaning of apprehension
Or fear—back in those days when it was you
They treated well.

ANATH [*in the tent-opening*]. Does he still not apprehend
Or fear?

SHENDI. Madam, madam—

ANATH.   What are you doing
To Egypt, Moses?

MOSES.   What have you come for?

ANATH.   You.
  What are you doing to Egypt, Moses?

MOSES.   What
  Is Egypt doing to Egypt?

ANATH.   Or Egypt to you.
  Come with me. I came by the old walks.
  What have I seen? You shall come with me
  And see it and tell me, and see the men and women
  Bewildered in the doorways, for the name of their world
  Has changed from home to horror. And is this
  What you have in your heart for Egypt? Then favour me
  And also have it in your eyes.

MOSES.   But why
  Do you come to me? To whose blood has the Nile
  Turned? It isn't mine. Can it be the spilt blood
  Of Israelites that is flowing back on Egypt?
  Why come to me?

ANATH.   He wants reason! Rationalize
  The full moon and the howling dog. I have less
  Inclination to be here than the dog has to howl.
  If you come with me to Seti, he's ready to talk to you.

MOSES. We've talked already.

ANATH.   He'll let you take your Hebrews
  To make their worship, or whatever you want of them,
  On some conditions which he'll tell you.

AARON.   Good.
  Events are moving.

MOSES.   If Seti is so ready,
  Why did you make the walk through the ominous evening
  To remind me that I'm in Egypt?

ANATH.   Because he is sitting
  Pressing his thumbs together, wedged inactive
  In between his decision and pride. What it is
  To have to do with men! They live too large.
  I'm ready to take you.

MOSES. I'll go.

AARON.   This will be a great day for Israel.

MIRIAM. My son has been made an officer.

ANATH.   I shall be glad
  Not to be alone this time, with the earth
  Wavering to a hint of doom. I suppose
  There have to be powers of darkness, but they should keep
  To the rules. The sky is lighter. The worst may be over.

MOSES. Aaron, you will come too.

AARON.   It has been easier
  Than I should have thought possible this morning.

                       [*Exeunt* ANATH, MOSES, *and* AARON

SHENDI. What is this business the Pharaoh has with my uncle?

MIRIAM. I mustn't think of Moses. Many things
  I must be sure to keep my thoughts quite away from.
  What is it we have to do? A dark mind
  And he has followed that woman.

SHENDI. Will he try to stop my commission going through?

MIRIAM. No, no, he's forgotten it.

SHENDI.   What does he matter, then?
  I'm an officer!

MIRIAM.   How could the water be blood, Shendi?

SHENDI. What?

MIRIAM.   I'll put your things together for you.
How grand we shall be!

CURTAIN

SCENE TWO

A room in the Palace. SETI. ANATH.

ANATH. Keep the window covered, Seti. The terrace
Crackles with dying locusts. I looked out.
I seemed to look within, on to myself,
When I stood there and looked out over Egypt.
The face of all this land is turned to the wall.
I looked out, and when I looked to the north I saw
Instead of quiet cattle, glutted jackals,
Not trees and pasture but vulture-bearing boughs
And fields which had been sown with hail. And looking
To the south I saw, like falling ashes after fire,
Death after thirst, death after hunger, death
After disease. And when I looked to the east
I saw an old woman ridding herself of lice;
And to the west, a man who had no meaning
Pushing thigh-deep through drifts of locusts.

SETI. Well; these things are finished.

ANATH.   And what happens
Now? What will you do when the mourners have done
Wailing, and men look across the havoc of their fields
And the bones of their cattle and say: You did this,
What happens now?

SETI.   Why am I to be blamed
  For all the elemental poisons that come up fungoid
  Out of the damps and shadows which our existence
  Moves in? Can I put peace into the furious
  God-epilepsy of earthquake and eruption?
  What am I but one of those you pity?

ANATH. You tricked him, you tricked Moses, and not once
  But seven times. First when I, against
  All my self-warning, approached the unapproachable
  And brought him to you. Didn't you make him promises
  Then, and break them? And that night your promises
  Plagued our ears with a croaking mockery,
  With an unceasing frog-echo of those words
  Which had meant nothing; with a plague of frogs!
  A second time you made promises, and a third time
  And a fourth: seven times you've broken them
  While the stews of creation had their way with Egypt.

SETI. You say this, concoct this legend; you have become
  Infected with the venom that's against me.

ANATH. No, I've no venom. I've no more efficacy
  Than a fishwife who has been made to breed against
  Her will; and so I'm shrill and desperate.
  No power against misery! That's what our lives add up to.
  Our spacious affability, our subtle intelligence,
  Our delicate consciousness of worlds beyond the world,
  Our persuasive dignity when sacrificing to the gods,
  Our bodies and our brains can all become
  Slutted with lice between afternoon and evening.
  You tricked him a second time, and that is what
  You saw: sweet made foul. And then the third time
  And we became the dungheap, the lusted of flies,
  The desirable excretion. Our pleasantness was flyblown.

SETI. I've suffered this once with Egypt—

ANATH.   You tricked Moses.
  And what has come of it I would bring back to you
  Until pity came out of you like blood to the knife,
  Remembering how disease swept all the cattle,
  How we could not sleep for intolerable lowing
  Till daylight rounded up the herds of wolftorn
  Death. You tricked him, and that feculent moment
  Filthied our blood and made of us a nation
  Loathsome with boils. You had stirred up the muck
  Which the sweet gods thought fit to make us of
  When they first formed man, the primal putrescence
  We keep hidden under our thin dress of health.
  What a pretty world, this world of filthmade kings!
  When, after the sixth time, the hail came down,
  I laughed. The hail was hard, metallic, cold
  And clean, beating on us with the ferocity
  Of brainbright anger. As cut diamonds, clean,
  Clean, and fit to be beaten down by. When
  It stamped out the gardens and cracked the skulls of birds
  It bruised away the memory of vermin
  And struck our faces fairly. If then, if only
  Then our consciousness had gone clean out,
  Or if then you had let these Israelites go with Moses,
  We should not now so vainly
  Shuffle our fingers in the dust to find
  The name we once were known by. But you tricked
  For the seventh time, and then the curse of the locusts
  Strangled the whole air, the whole earth,
  Devoured the last leaf of the old life
  That we had sometime lived. The land is naked
  To the bone, and men are naked beyond the bone,

Down to the barest nakedness which until now
Hope kept covered up. Now climb and sit
On the throne of this reality, and be
A king.

SETI.   Anath! These plagues were not my doing
And you know they were not. No man would say I caused them.
Only a woman with her mind hung
With a curtain of superstition would say so.

ANATH.   I admit it.
I am superstitious. I have my terrors.
We are born too inexplicably out
Of one night's pleasure, and have too little security:
No more than a beating heart to keep us probable.
There must be other probabilities.
You tricked Moses after I had gone myself
To bring him to you, and what followed followed.

SETI. It is true I made certain concessions to Moses
And reconsidered them. I was prepared
To let him have his way, if in return
He would use his great abilities to our advantage.
But am I to have no kind of surety
That he'll return, after this godhunt of his?
I said to him Take the men but their wives and children
Must remain. And then I went further: I told him to take
Both men and women, but the children must stay. And at last
I only insisted on their cattle, since our cattle
Were dead. I'll not be panicked by this chain
Of black coincidence, which he with his genius
For generalship has taken advantage of.
He presumes upon the eternal because he has
No power to strike his bargain. I have not done
These things to Egypt. I'll not hear it be said.

ANATH. Well, they're done. Blame has no value anyway.
There's not one of us whose life doesn't make mischief
Somewhere. Now after all you've had to give in.
At last, this morning, he has carried the day.
We must calculate again, calculate without Moses.
I picked unhappy days in those girlhood rushes.
But at least we can sweep away the locusts.

SETI. How carried the day? It is he
Who must calculate again. You understand
There will be no postponement of Rameses' marriage;
We can look forward to that, and the happy outcome
Of my careful policy.

ANATH.   What do you mean?
Moses by now has called the assembly of the Hebrews.
By now Egypt has heard the news. Moses
Has taken policy out of your hands.

SETI.   I sent
Word after him.

ANATH.   Seti! What word did you send?
What have you done?

SETI.   I have only been careful
To protect your future. Even before Moses
Had gone three steps from the palace there came the news
Of another defeat. Fate has taken a hammer
To chip and chip at our confidence.
But while I still have Moses to come at my call
I have not lost him. And while he needs my help
He will continue to come. And when he is tired—
We'll make a bargain.

ANATH.   All this, then, over again.
You're mad. It isn't we who make the bargains
In this life, but chance and time. I tell you it's madness!

Enter RAMESES

RAMESES. Father,
Is it true you've withdrawn your latest promise to Moses?

SETI. Whatever I have done or not done isn't to be said
In a sentence.

RAMESES.   They say it's true. Wherever I have gone
Dank rumour has been rising off the pavements, chilling
Into the heart of the people: 'Pharaoh has refused
Moses again. What new disastrous day
Is coming?' I tell you I've been out walking
Under the burning windows of the people's eyes.
You've stood fast long enough. Let Moses take
The Hebrews.

SETI.   So you also are afraid of magic
And believe that this tall Moses can make a business
Out of curses? Do you suppose if I surrendered to him
There would be any less roaring in the wind
Or less infection in disease? Why
Aren't you beside me like another man,
Instead of so fretting me with nursery behaviour
That I could strike you? I made life in your mother
To hand me strength when I should need it. That life
Was you. I made you exactly for this time
And I find you screeching to escape it.

RAMESES.   I have been
Through streets that no men should have to walk in.
You must let the Hebrews go. Father, you must!

SETI. You know nothing, you little fool, nothing! Govern
By your idiocy when I am dead.

RAMESES.   What
  Will you leave for me to govern, or what by then
  Shall I have become, what figure of faded purple
  Who clears his throat on an unimportant throne?
  I am to you only the boy who comes
  To the door to say goodnight on his way to bed.
  It's you who invite the future but it's I
  Who have to entertain it, remember that.
  What is expedience for you may become
  Dark experience for me. And these last weeks
  I've heard the future's loping footfall, as plague
  Came after plague, and I knew the steps
  Were not passing but approaching. You
  Were persuading them. They came each time a little
  Nearer, and each time closer to me.
  Keep your word to Moses. Let him take them.
SETI. I tell you it isn't possible.

RAMESES.   Then get
  Yourself another heir, and make him eat
  Your black bread of policy. Marry yourself
  To this girl from Syria. My plans are different.
SETI. Your plans are different! You insolent cub, you spoiled
  Insolent cub! And so your plans are different?
  You've already made your plans!

RAMESES.   Wait. What
  Was that noise?
ANATH.   The old familiar. A man crying out.
  What difference is one man's groaning more or less?
RAMESES [*looking from the terrace*]. Oh horrible! What is it that
    makes men
  And makes them like this man? Abortions of nature.
  It is true what they said.

ANATH.   What is true?

RAMESES. What the other officers said, what I thought they spread
About out of malice: that Shendi outstruts them all,
Drives the Hebrews harder than any Egyptian
Drives them, hits them down with a readier fist,
And smiles and thrives under the admiration
Of the overseers. Go out on the terrace if you doubt me
And see him, Shendi, the son of Miriam, a Jew
Beating a Jew.

SETI.   So perhaps at last,
So perhaps at last you will have seen
That what you thought was child's play, black and white,
Is a problem of many sides. And you will kindly
Wait and learn. This fellow does the work
Which you yourself suggested he should do
And does it conscientiously, without sentiment.

RAMESES. I suggested he should do it. Yes.
I put the whip in his hand. I raised that arm.
I struck that Jew. I did it. I did not know
How the things we do, take their own life after
They are done, how they can twist themselves
Into foul shapes. I can now see better
The deathly ground we live on. Yes, all right,
I have surrendered. Whatever happens will happen
Without me. I've finished meddling.

ANATH.   Rameses!
Of all the Jews one Jew has done this.

RAMESES.   It might be
A thousand instead of one.

ANATH.   Rameses, only
One Jew!

SETI. Would you even encourage the traitor
In my son, because of your fear of this Moses?

ANATH.   Yes,
I would make him rebellious, and if I could I would make
Every limb of your body rebellious;
I'd paralyse that pride which sends us packing
Into a daily purgatory of apprehension.

SETI. Turn yourselves all against me.
I stand now living and breathing only to protect
This country from disintegration.

ANATH.   Oh
The gods, how we fumble between right and wrong,
Between our salvation and our overthrow,
Like drunk men with a key in the dark who stand
At the right door but cannot get out of the cold.
May the moment of accident bless us.

RAMESES.   I shall not
Rebel again. That will be one trouble less.

SETI. Stand beside me. We're almost of equal height
And may yet come to be of equal mind;
And if that is so, one of us will find
The way of escape out of this distress
Of ours, either you or I.

                Enter KEF, *a Minister to the Pharaoh*

KEF.   My lord Pharaoh.

SETI. News; come on.

KEF.   Better to hear it alone.

SETI. Bad news. Well, let's have it. Catastrophe
Is no longer my secret. Let us have it all.

KEF. My lord—

SETI.   Go on, go on.

KEF.   A report that the Libyans
Have annihilated the reinforcing fifth
Division.

SETI.   It is impossible.

KEF.   They were surrounded
And surprised. Only six men got through.

SETI.   Six men.

RAMESES. Six men.

SETI.   They load me to the last inch.

Enter TEUSRET

TEUSRET.   Moses has come
Again. I saw him walking like a lion
Behind bars, up and down in your battered garden,
Rameses. The sentries had tried to hold him
But he broke through their spears as though he didn't see them.
He looked at me, his eyes the colour of anger;
He looked at me and gripped a mulberry-bough
And broke it, and said Go to your father, fetch me
Your father.

SETI.   He can walk longer and break more boughs.
He shall wait, and find that Egypt is hard ground
Under his lion's walk. [*To* KEF] Go out to the overseers
And tell them to tighten discipline, to give
No rest to those Hebrews, not to let man, woman
Or child straighten their backs while they still stand.
I shall not see him until I choose; and, when
I choose, for his people's sake, he'll do what I need.
See this done.

ANATH.   Seti, take care; take care
What you do.

SETI.   Let Moses think again what behaviour
Is best, best to save his people.   [*Exit*

TEUSRET.   Rameses,
What is it? Why are you so silent? Are you afraid
As well? Are you afraid? Are you, Rameses?

RAMESES. Why should I be? The sweet part of the world's
All over, but that's nothing. It had to go.
My mind had lutes and harps and nodding musicians
Who drowned my days with their casual tunes. They have been
Paid off by this honest hour. And now I hear
My voice raised in deathly quiet. It's insufferable
That my voice, without the accompaniment of good fortune,
Should be so out of key, so faltering,
So cracking with puberty.—Aunt Anath,
What's the meaning of my manhood, to be found
So helpless, to be so helpless: what is there to do
Which I could do and haven't yet seen?

ANATH. We're no longer alone.

                          [MOSES *stands in the doorway*

TEUSRET.   Look, Rameses.

MOSES.   Where is Seti?

ANATH. He will not see you.

MOSES.   When will he learn? When,
When, when will he learn? We have agonized
This land with anger for too many days.

ANATH.   You
And he together. No birth is worth this labour.

MOSES. For three hundred years the pangs of this coming deliver-
        ance
    Have been suffered by my people, while Egypt played.
    But now Egypt suffers, and she says
    This is a new hell. But hell is old;
    And you yourself sitting in sunlight
    Embroidered on it with your needle. Hell
    Is old, but until now
    It fed on other women, that is all.

ANATH. And all is the innocent as well as the guilty;
    All is the small farmer and the singing fisherman
    And the wife who sweeps; tomorrow's boy as well
    As yesterday's. All these, while Seti twists
    To have his way, must go to your fire like sticks.

RAMESES [*looking from the terrace*]. The gods help them now! The
        gods help those Hebrews!

MOSES. It must be one people or another, your people
    Or mine. You appeal to Moses,
    But Moses is now only a name and an obedience.
    It is the God of the Hebrews, a vigour moving
    In a great shadow, who draws the bow
    Of his mystery, to loose this punishing arrow
    Feathered with my fate; he who in his hour
    Broke the irreparable dam which kept his thought,
    Released the cataract of birth and death
    To storm across time and the world;
    He who in his morning
    Drew open the furious petals of the sun;
    He who through his iron fingers
    Lets all go, lets all waste and go,
    Except, dearly retained in his palm, the soul:

He, the God of my living, the God of the Hebrews,
Has stooped beside Israel
And wept my life like a tear of passion
On to the iniquity of Egypt.

ANATH. So the great general steps down to captaincy.
I wonder. Does this god use you
Or do you use this god? What is this divinity
Which with no more dexterity than a man
Rips up good things to make a different kind
Of good? For any god's sake, if you came here
To get justice, also give justice.
In this mood the lot goes headlong.

MOSES.   Headlong!
And our memories too. And our hands which once
Knew how to come together, must now for ever
Hide themselves in our dress. We are utterly separate.

RAMESES. Look at the sky! A sea of cloud, blind-black,
Is pouring on to the beaches of the sun!

TEUSRET. Oh, it will swamp the sailing of the air!
The sky will be gone from us, it's taking the sky!
What shall we do?

ANATH.   Hush, Teusret.

                                   [*The stage grows dark*

MOSES.   Seti
May see better without the light of day.
The hand of God has gone across his eyes
And closed all life upon itself. Egypt
Goes inward, by a gate which shuts more heavily than sunset,

Leaving man alone with his baffled brain.
Only Seti can let the sun free again.

ANATH. It is here! The darkness!

MOSES.   Tell him, tell Seti
That I wait for his answer.

CURTAIN TO ACT TWO

ACT THREE

SCENE ONE

MIRIAM'S *tent at night.* AARON. *Enter* MIRIAM.

AARON. Everything has been done, I think. I have daubed
    The lamb's blood three times over the entry
    And all that remained of the meat has been burned.—
    Miriam! You; not Moses! What do you want
    Here at close on midnight?

MIRIAM.   Must I want something
    To come into my own tent?

AARON.   Tell me; what is it?
    There's no time left. Has the news got past our silence?
    Do they know? That's why you've come in the night. The
        Egyptians
    Are one ahead of us!

MIRIAM.   News? I've got no news.
    Is there any news at midnight? I've come to sleep.

AARON. Why not sleep, as you did, in the city with Shendi?

MIRIAM. Do I have to be catechized in my own tent?
    If you want to ferret in unlighted places
    Penetrate into the mind of Moses, and let me
    Sleep.

AARON. His mind will be our history
    Before the morning. Whatever is about to happen—
    I cannot doubt that something is about to happen—
    Will divulge him to us at last. I have become

Almost docile to his darkness. By what providence
I wonder, did you come back? There was no way
Of getting word to you, but you came, thank God.
Whatever is wrong for you, to make you walk
So far to sleep, this midnight of Moses
(I call it to myself his midnight) will clarify
Into right.

MIRIAM.   Wrong things and right things!
So you still talk of those, those things that are catches
To make us lose heart. Take evil by the tail
And you find you are holding good head-downwards.
Let me go to sleep.

AARON.   Something that Shendi has done
Has brought you back.

MIRIAM.   Shendi, Shendi to blame!
To you Shendi is always blameable.
Because at last he can have ambitions,
Because he's ripping up the bare boards
His boyhood lay on, to make himself a fire
Which will warm his manhood, we turn on him—yes,
I also, as much as you—I stormed so.
I? The right to blame him? The wrong to have borne him
To that childhood. Why shouldn't he be finished with the lot of
    us?

AARON. So he turned you out: he sent you away.

MIRIAM.   I left him.
I came away from him. I couldn't watch him
Live what is now his life.

AARON.   I won't think of him.

MIRIAM. He'll succeed without your thoughts.

AARON.   Look at me, Miriam.

MIRIAM. You're going away.

AARON.   And so is all Israel.
We all have staves in our hands and our feet shod
For travelling; Moses' orders. He also gave
Other orders; they were very curious.
We have all had to eat lambs' flesh, seasoned
With bitter herbs. As I see it, Miriam,
That is his characteristic way of achieving
Unity among us, before the event,
That we should all fill this waiting time by doing
The same thing, however trivial. And then
We have splashed the blood three times over the doorways.
That is quite inexplicable. It is drying in the night air,
At this moment, while I speak. What happens, I ask myself,
When it is dry? It means our freedom. He has told me so.
Tonight we're to go free. And when I look at him
I have to permit myself a wonderful hope.

MIRIAM. He came back from Midian a madman.

AARON. His madness seems to be a kind of extended sanity.
But he tells me nothing, nothing is discussed or planned
Even with me, his lieutenant. And this closeness
Has hurt me, I won't try to deny it. And yet
He has me by the scruff of the heart and I ask
No questions. I've begun to believe that the reasonable
Is an invention of man, altogether in opposition
To the facts of creation, though I wish it hadn't
Occurred to me. I've been with Moses, watching
How in tent after tent he manipulated
Man upon man into consciousness. Though perhaps
They don't know of what they're conscious, any more than I do.
Except of the night; of the night, Miriam! I would swear
The night is dedicated to our cause.

                                                    E

You must have seen it: there's such a brightness,
Such a swingeing stillness, the sky has transfixed itself;
As though it hung with every vigorous star
On some action to be done before daybreak.

Enter SHENDI

SHENDI. Why must he be here?
I have something to say to you, mother.

MIRIAM.   Not any more
Tonight; nothing more said tonight. Go back
To your bed.

SHENDI.   Yes, you must listen!

AARON.   Listen to your tongue
Or your brotherly whip?

MIRIAM.   He knows already what we feel.
Now let him alone.

SHENDI.   Let him think what he likes. I have come
To you, not to him. We've taken so long to get
What at last we have: why must you spoil it? I know;
It was the spate of our tempers, gone again now.
If you go away from me, more than half the triumph
Is lost. You haven't been my mother for nothing.
I mean to see you happy.

MIRIAM.   I shall stay alone.

SHENDI. Oh, it's fantastic. What did you expect
My work to be? And how can we be scrupulous
In a life which, from birth onwards, is so determined
To wring us dry of any serenity at all?

MIRIAM. You must do as you must.

AARON.   But in the morning
He may wish he had chosen otherwise.

SHENDI.   What do you mean?
  Let me hear what you mean by that. Have you
  And your brother done some dirtiness against me
  To put me wrong with the Pharaoh? I know you'd founder me
  If you had the chance——

                    Enter MOSES

MOSES.   Get ready, Miriam. And you,
  Shendi. Get together all that you value.
  You won't come to this tent again.

MIRIAM.   Get ready?
  All that I value? What would that be, I wonder?
  Tell your delirium to be precise.

AARON. This midnight is his. For pity's sake believe it,
  Miriam. Then all our wills resolved into
  One Will——

SHENDI.   His, of course! The stupendous mischief
  Of the man! I beg your pardon if he no longer
  Rates himself as a man after living through
  The pestilences as though he owned them.
  You can blame him, not me, for the punishment
  I give the labourers. He makes them undisciplined
  With his raving of freedom which they'll never get.
  It's he, not I, who knits the darker and darker
  Frowns for Pharaoh—it's he who's the one for you
  To abominate, if anybody.

MOSES.   Be ready for journey.
  The time is prepared for us. What we were is sinking
  Under the disposition of what will be.
  Let it so dispose; let us not fondle our wrongs
  Because they're familiar. Now, as the night turns,

A different life, pitched above our experience
Or imagining, is moving about its business.
Tonight—Aaron, Miriam, Shendi—our slavery
Will be gone.

AARON.   Do you hear what he says?

MIRIAM.   What is he hiding?
There's something he knows.

AARON.   Something known by the night;
That was how it felt to me.

MIRIAM.   What is it you know?

MOSES.   The sound
Of God. It comes; after all, it comes. It made
The crucial interchange of earth with everlasting;
Found and parted the stone lips of this
Egyptian twilight in the speech of souls,
Moulding the air of all the world, and desiring
Into that shell of shadow, a man's mind—
Into my own.

AARON.   What was told? What was said?

SHENDI.   Oh, leave them
To excite each other. I'm going if you're not.

MOSES. Stay where you are. Do you deny voice
To that power, the whirler of suns and moons, when even
Dust can speak, as it does in Moses now?
It comes.
And by the welding of what loved me and what harmed me,
I have been brought to that stature which has heard.
Tonight, at midnight,
God will unfasten the hawk of death from his
Grave wrist, to let it rake our world,

Descend and obliterate the firstborn of Egypt,
All the firstborn, cattle, flocks, and men:
Mortality lunging in the midnight fields
And briding in the beds: a sombre visit
Such as no nation has known before. Upon
All Egypt! Only we who have the darkness
Here in our blood, under the symbol of blood
Over our doors, only we of Israel
Standing ready for the morning will be unvisited.

AARON. So this is what you know.

SHENDI.   What he wants, what he fondly
  Imagines. Why did I follow you here
  To get drawn into this? That fox has his tail on fire
  And someone should know about it. For the last time,
  Are you coming?

MIRIAM.   Don't go back—not just
  Within a pace of this midnight.

SHENDI.   I can see
  What's been thought out between you. Now that you have me,
  You think you'll keep me: here, dropped back in the pit.
  What chance of it! Must I tell you that I'm an Egyptian?
  An Egyptian! I'm an Egyptian!

AARON.   Mind what you say, Shendi!
  Remember the midnight promised to us,
  Which is almost here! No doubt the timing of God
  Will be extremely exact. And does nothing, no presentiment,
  Creep on the heart of Pharaoh at this moment?

MOSES. Aaron!

AARON. I wonder, does nothing make him fetch his firstborn
  Beside him——

MOSES.   Aaron!
  Do you see the ambush I have blundered into?
  I heard God, as though hearing were understanding.
  But he kept his hands hidden from me. He spoke,
  But while he spoke he pointed. Aaron, he pointed
  At Rameses, and I couldn't see!

AARON.   The boy
  Pays for the father.

MOSES.   Why had I not thought of him?—
  When other boys were slaughtered I was spared for Israel.
  Surely I who have been the go-between for God
  Can keep one firstborn living now for Egypt?

AARON. Is this how you fought your other wars?
  There were boys then who put
  Eager toes into fatal stirrups, who were young
  And out of life altogether in the same
  Almighty and unthinkable moment. You learnt
  Then to grieve and advance, uninterrupted.
  And so it has to be now.

MOSES.   Look what it is,
  God is putting me back with the assassins.
  Is that how he sees me? I killed an Egyptian
  And buried him in the sand. Does one deed then
  Become our immortal shape? And Egypt! Egypt!
  He was meant for Egypt. Aaron,
  You are here in my place until I come again.
  Keep Shendi with you.

AARON.   Where are you going?

MOSES. Keep Shendi with you.   [*He goes*

AARON. He is in a space somewhere between
The human and inhuman. That's a terrible
Neighbourhood.

SHENDI.   Did you see how he looked? He believes
What he said.

MIRIAM.   Shut us in. He has gone.
Can't we forget the man?

SHENDI.   I won't stay here!
Thank goodness I can go where things are healthier.

AARON. It's midnight.
Wasn't that the winding of the city's horn,
The sound of twelve? I think so. I have to delay you,
Shendi.

SHENDI [*at the tent-opening*]. Nobody will delay me.

MIRIAM.   Stay in the tent!

AARON. The hour may go past and leave us knowing
It was unremarkable. But wait till the light,
Wait, Shendi, keep yourself unseen
By that inquisition of stars out there.
Wait for Moses to return.

SHENDI.   Who?

MIRIAM. What is it? What have you seen?

SHENDI.   I've lost the city,
I can't reach it! You trapped me!

MIRIAM.   What do you see?

SHENDI. The sand is rising and living!
Is an invisible nation going through to the north?
Or what is it the sand can feel? I can't go back,
God, God, I can't go!

MIRIAM.   Come inside,
  Shendi, come into the tent.

AARON.   Happening,
  You see, happening. Why try to go back?

SHENDI. Some of the men will still be awake. We could light
  The lights in the barrack-room. If only some of them
  Would come out to look for me! Can you hear it, the noise,
  The rending apart and shuddering-to of wings?
  Where can I get away from this? Nowhere
  Except into the ground.

MIRIAM.   Shendi, here, in the tent.
  In the tent: it will pass the tent.

AARON [*dragging him in*].   Are you trying to die?

SHENDI. Let me go, death; death, let me go!

AARON.
  Not death.

SHENDI.   It isn't only you.
  The wings were right over me and I was wrenched by a hand
  That came spinning out of them. I'll not be sent into a grave.
  I'll be what I was. I am Shendi, a Jew.
  How can my blood alter and make me Egyptian?
  I only wanted to be free!   [*He tears off the Egyptian uniform*
  Look: Egypt comes away—it's no part of me,
  It's easily off. This body is all I am—
  It is Shendi, the Jew, Shendi, Shendi, a Jew,
  A Jew! Isn't it so? Then why am I dying?

MIRIAM. You are not, Shendi; it's gone past us. There's nothing
  more.

AARON. Look, you're with us.

SHENDI.   Only free to die?
This wasn't a world. It was death from the beginning.
Here's my name, without a man to it. My name!
Let me go. It's a chance! I'll make them see me. Wings,

>   [*He breaks away into the dark*

Shadows, eagles! I am Shendi, Shendi, the Jew!
I am Shendi the Jew! Shendi the Jew!

MIRIAM.   Shendi!
He has gone behind the sand. Son!   [*She runs into the dark*

AARON.   The night
Of deliverance. Tonight we all go free.
And Miriam too. He said she would go free.

>   [*The voice of* MIRIAM *is heard crying out her last desperate*
>   '*Shendi!*'

CURTAIN

SCENE TWO

The Palace. ANATH. TEUSRET

ANATH. How the stars have taken possession of the sky tonight.

TEUSRET. Occasion, dear Aunt. Phipa is coming,
The magnitude out of Syria.

ANATH.   Tomorrow.

TEUSRET. No; now they say tonight, very soon,
For Rameses. Messengers were here
Half an hour ago, sweating in the cool yard.
She's already at Hahiroth, with her romantic nature
Plying the spurs, and waking all the villages

With the interminable jingle-jangle of what father calls
Her considerable means. We shall see her tonight.

ANATH. How do we welcome her? Nothing has been said
To me.

TEUSRET. Who says anything in this palace now
Except good morning or good night? Father
Waits for each moment to come and touch him
And then it has gone before he can use it.

ANATH.   And you
Have a hard welcome for this girl from Syria.

TEUSRET. No; I'm praying her here, for all our sakes.
She will bring solid and gay Syria
To chase away the fiends.

Enter SETI

Who is that?

SETI. I. Is there something to be seen?

ANATH. We're watching the dark for bridles.

TEUSRET.   And the dark
Watches us. I know you dislike me to be afraid of it.
Are we all to meet her in the jumping shadows,
Aunts, owls, flame, sisters and all?
Or will she go quietly to bed and wait for tomorrow?

SETI. Tonight. She must dismount into a light
Of welcome. Where's your brother? . . . Turn this way;
Are you handsome? Well, the years of my life
Conveyed in a woman, perhaps safely. Remember to love me
For everything you become, particularly
For the worship of the male sunrise which will stand
Over your maturity.

TEUSRET. What is it, father?
What is it?

SETI. How many thousand thousand years
Are being nursed in your body, my young daughter?
And under a secure lock, away from the eyes.

TEUSRET. What eyes?

SETI. The envy; confusion.
Where's Rameses?

TEUSRET. In bed.

SETI. He can go to bed tomorrow.

ANATH. Precious heart,
That was a wild cry that ripped the darkness
From somewhere down in the city.

SETI. He will have dreams in plenty after tonight;
I'm giving them to him with both my hands. Where is he?
Fetch him.

RAMESES [*in the doorway*]. I am here, sir.

SETI. You're the Pharaoh.

ANATH. Seti!

SETI. You have slept into a throne and an empire
While time has begun to heap age over me
With a bony spade, to make me like the rest,
Rameses, like the poor rest.

RAMESES. Has Syria come?

ANATH. Tell the boy what you mean: and me.
What are you pulling down now?

SETI. Myself.
It seems that I have grown too tall
And keep out the sun. I overbranch the light.

I am giving you the throne, Rameses.
It gives itself. The wind has hurled it under you,
A biting wind, the hatred that has turned me
Into decay and grub in my own garden.
You may have luckier hands. You have at least
Hands less calloused with enemies. You will be able
To hold the sceptre perhaps without such pain.

ANATH. Abdication!

RAMESES.   Is that what you mean? The throne?

SETI. This is how we distract them: under my seal
Affixed in the morning, Moses shall have the permission
He has raged for: and then, with the sun somewhat higher,
Under my final seal you shall take Egypt.
I drown myself in my own wave: I am not,
But I am always. And when they come, the factions,
The whorers and devourers, roaring over
The rocks of the dynasty, they'll only find
Perpetual Egypt.

RAMESES.   I'm to inherit the kingdom
Of desperate measures, to be not a self
But a glove disguising your hand. Is there nowhere
Where I can come upon my own shape
Between these overbearing ends of Egypt?
Where am I to look for life?

SETI.   What else
Am I shaking over you but a wealth of life?
Do you comprehend, this land, the bright wrists
Of the world on which the centuries are bracelets,
Is yours? And the heart of beauty out of Syria.
Teusret, watch: is there anything to be seen?
Any sound yet?—Stupidity, what would you have?

Love is the dominant of life, to which all our changes
Of key are subdued in the end. You will be able
To wander the winding and coitous passages
Of the heart, and be more than you could have prophesied
For yourself.

TEUSRET.　　Listen, listen!

SETI.　　　　　　　Is it the girl?

TEUSRET. No, listen!

ANATH.　　　　A tortured gale, a gale
Of crying moving through the streets.

TEUSRET.　　　　　　　Listen!
It's the noise of breaking lives.

SETI.　　　　　　What is it now?

RAMESES. What is it, Darkness? Why are you coming now?
For whom this time?

ANATH.　　　　Oh, make the city silent!

TEUSRET. Someone's coming: a shadow, a man,
Leaping for the terrace.

RAMESES.　　　　Let it come to me.
If I'm to have Egypt I'll have its treachery, too.
Keep away from the window. Who goes there? Stand.
Who goes there? Who is it?

[MOSES *comes breathlessly on to the terrace*

MOSES. Shut all your doors! Nothing will wait for us,
We are at war with this moment. Draw yourselves
Like swords. It is for Rameses.

RAMESES.　　　　For me?

MOSES. Put your lives round him.

SETI.   Have you come
  Out of the city? What's there? What's on its way?

MOSES. Death, death, deliberately
  Aimed, falling on all your firstborn sons,
  All Egypt's firstborn, Seti, cattle and men;
  Death mounting with a growing storm of cries
  To your window, to come to Rameses. I know—
  It was I that loosed it. Can I deflect it now?
  Can we so rope our lives together that we
  Can be a miracle against death?

SETI.   Go back
  Into your night. I'll not believe in you.

ANATH. What do you want from us?

MOSES.   Power of life
  To beat death out of this house.
  The vigour of our lives must be
  The miracle to save him.

ANATH.   What is my life?
  It went to be your shadow. For fifteen years
  It has been nothing but a level of darkness
  Cast on the world by you. I made myself
  Your mother, and then loved you and desired you
  Till you became the best and worst of the world,
  The water that kept me alive to thirst.

MOSES. Anath——

ANATH.   I loved you until I longed to hear
  That you were dead.

MOSES.   Not this, not now!
  Give me greater life for the boy's sake.

SETI. There is no more life to be demanded of me
Than I've already given: care,
Effort, devotion, sacrifice of all inclination,
Even to the sacrifice of my own person.
I have changed the channel that evil was running in.
This boy's the Pharaoh now.

RAMESES.   And yet,
If I'm to live, shall I know how?

MOSES. We'll hold you with our lives, if our lives will hold.
More life! The dark is already beside us.
In life's name, what are we?
Five worlds of separation? Or can we be
Five fingers to close into a hand
To strike this death clean away from us?
Has none of us the life to keep him living?

SETI. A great power, a great people,
A living Egypt.

MOSES.   Pain of man,
Affirm my strength, and make me
Equal to this wrestler come against me.

TEUSRET. Look, look—the torches in the gateway;
She is here!

SETI.   Anath, all of you,
We meet her as though Egypt were in high health;
No anxiety on your faces as though you were ambassadors
Of some haunted country.

TEUSRET.   We shall be alive again.
Phipa has come to us, and the horns have begun
To wind their welcome in the towers. Come on,

Rameses, come to meet her. The dark's not dangerous
Now.

RAMESES. But still dark. And we have to enact
A daylight for this unsuspecting beauty.
Well, we'll meet her.

ANATH.   No, don't go, don't look!
The men who were opening the gates to let her in
Have fallen to the ground. An owl in mid-air
Has wrenched itself upward screaming, and smashed
Down to the yard—there falls another! Oh,
Are these the flowers we throw at her feet?
You asked us for life, Moses; what life have you
Against this death which pushes through the gate
Shoulder to shoulder with the bride? Moses,
It is now that you must break through to your power,
Now! It's here.

MOSES.   The shadows are too many.
All was right, except this, all, the reason,
The purpose, the justice, except this culmination.
Good has turned against itself and become
Its own enemy. Have we to say that truth
Is only punishment? What must we say
To be free of the bewildering mesh of God?
Where is my hand to go to? Rameses,
There's no more of me than this. This is all:
I followed a light into a blindness.

TEUSRET.   Come
Away, Rameses, Rameses, come now.
You must meet her and love her.
Isn't it in love that life is strongest?
I want you to love her. Already we're late.

RAMESES. Why is she sighing, Teusret? Such great sighs.
They have taken all the air. Now there will be
Nowhere to breathe. Come with me.

[*He crumples and falls*

TEUSRET.   Rameses,
I don't know the way!

RAMESES.   I am finding it for you.
Stoop, Teusret. You see? You cannot lose me.
Here I am. [*He dies.*]

TEUSRET.   Where? Where? Rameses!
I'll meet her alone, then. When she comes she'll reach you.
She must, she must. She came so far.

[*She runs to the courtyard*

ANATH. Rameses, pharaoh of sleep, you have
The one sure possession of the world.

SETI [*to* MOSES]. You have done what you returned for.
You found us in the morning.
Leave us with what remains of the night.
The day you found us in is over.

Enter AARON

AARON. We are standing ready. The sound of the wings is quiet
And the stars are fading in silence.
All ears wait for your command to march.
Egypt is throwing away its gold to have us gone.
Is it now?

MOSES.   Now! At last the crying of our past
Is over.

ANATH. You have the freedom of the darkness, Moses.
Why do you wait? Haven't you recognized
The triumph of your purpose? Your twelve hundred

Thousand souls, out there in the dungeon of the night,
Are waiting to hear the long bolts grate back.
Rameses has died,
And the air stands ready in the wilderness to take you in.
Rameses has died. Tomorrow the lizards
Will be sparkling on the rocks. Why aren't you dancing
With such liberty for such starving souls?

MOSES. Anath—Egypt,
Why was it I that had to be disaster to you?
I do not know why the necessity of God
Should feed on grief; but it seems so. And to know it
Is not to grieve less, but to see grief grow big
With what has died, and in some spirit differently
Bear it back to life. The blame could impale me
For ever; I could be so sick of heart
That who asked for my life should have it; or I could see
Man's life go forward only by guilt and guilt.
Then we should always be watching Rameses die.
Whereas he had such life his death can only
Take him for a moment, to undo his mortality,
And he is here pursuing the ends of the world.

ANATH. You have nothing now except the wilderness.

MOSES. The wilderness has wisdom.
And what does eternity bear witness to
If not at last to hope?

Re-enter TEUSRET

TEUSRET.   I have seen her. O Rameses,
She has come so gifted for you,
With pearls like seeds of the moon,
With metal and strange horns, ebon and ivory,
Spilling chalcedonyx and male sapphires.

Doesn't their brightness come to you? Do they glimmer
Nowhere into the cupboards of your sleep?

SETI. She need bring nothing, except the hour that has gone.

MOSES. Death and life are moving to a call.
I turn from Egypt.

ANATH.   What is left
To call to me?

MOSES.   The morning, which still comes
To Egypt as to Israel, the round of light
Which will not wheel in vain.
We must each find our separate meaning
In the persuasion of our days
Until we meet in the meaning of the world.
Until that time.

> [*He goes. The early light reaches* RAMESES

THE CURTAIN FALLS

THE PLAY ENDS

VENUS OBSERVED

A Comedy

TO PHYL

my wife

VENUS OBSERVED

*First produced by Sir Laurence Olivier at the
St. James's Theatre, London, on 18 January
1950*

The Duke of Altair	LAURENCE OLIVIER
Edgar	DENHOLM ELLIOTT
Herbert Reedbeck	GEORGE RELPH
Dominic	ROBERT BEAUMONT
Rosabel Fleming	VALERIE TAYLOR
Jessie Dill	BRENDA DE BANZIE
Captain Fox Reddleman	FRED JOHNSON
Bates	THOMAS HEATHCOTE
Hilda Taylor-Snell	RACHEL KEMPSON
Perpetua	HEATHER STANNARD

Décor by Roger Furse

CHARACTERS

(in order of their appearance)

THE DUKE OF ALTAIR

EDGAR, *his son*

HERBERT REEDBECK, *his agent*

DOMINIC, *Reedbeck's son*

ROSABEL FLEMING

JESSIE DILL

CAPTAIN FOX REDDLEMAN,
   the Duke's butler

BATES, *the Duke's footman*

HILDA TAYLOR-SNELL

PERPETUA, *Reedbeck's daughter*

SCENES

*The Observatory Room at Stellmere
Park, the Duke's mansion*

*The Temple of the Ancient Virtues,
Stellmere Park*

ACT ONE

*A room at the top of a mansion: once a bedroom, now an observatory.
When the curtain rises the* DUKE OF ALTAIR *is in argument
with his son* EDGAR. *Also present is* HERBERT REEDBECK, *the*
DUKE'S *agent.*

DUKE. Anyone would think I had made some extraordinary
Suggestion. But in fact how natural it is.
Aren't you my son?

EDGAR.   Yes, father, of course I am.

DUKE. Then it's up to you to choose who shall be your mother.
Does that seem to you improper, Reedbeck?

REEDBECK.   No,
Your Grace; it's not, perhaps, always done,
But few parents consider their children as you do.
I don't dislike the plan at all.

EDGAR.   I sweat
With embarrassment.

DUKE.   You have been
Too much with the horses. This, that I ask you to do,
Is an act of poetry, and a compliment
To the freshness of your mind. Why should you sweat?
Here they will be, three handsome women,
All of them at some time implicated
In the joyous routine of my life. (I could scarcely
Put it more delicately.) I wish to marry.
Who am I, in heaven's name, to decide
Which were my vintage years of love?

Good God, to differentiate between
The first bright blow on my sleeping flesh,
The big breasts of mid-morning,
And the high old dance of afternoon—
Value one against the other? Never, not I,
Till the eschatological rain shall lay my dust.
But you, dear boy, with your twenty-five impartial years,
Can perform the judgement of Paris,
Can savour, consider, and award the apple
With a cool hand. You will find an apple
Over there by the spectroscope.

EDGAR.   But why must you marry?
Or, if that's an impertinence, why do I have to have
A mother? I've been able to grow to a sizable boy
Without one.

DUKE.   Why? Because I see no end
To the parcelling out of heaven in small beauties,
Year after year, flocks of girls, who look
So lately kissed by God
They come out on the world with lips shining,
Flocks and generations, until time
Seems like nothing so much
As a blinding snowstorm of virginity,
And a man, lost in the perpetual scurry of white,
Can only close his eyes
In a resignation of monogamy.

EDGAR. Anyway, it would be an impossibly hasty
Judgement. Honour you as I may, I don't
See how I can do it.

DUKE.   If Paris had no trouble
Choosing between the tide-turning beauty,
Imponderable and sexed with eternity,

Of Aphrodite, Hera, and Athene,
Aren't you ashamed to make heavy weather of a choice
Between Hilda, and Rosabel, and Jessie?
And if you can't make up your mind about a woman
At first meeting, all hope of definition has gone;
Prejudice, delirium, or rage
Will cock their snooks, and the apple will go bad.
No, boy, no; go and water your horses
And come back and choose your mother.

EDGAR.   At what time?

DUKE. What is it now?

REEDBECK.   Five past eleven.

DUKE.   They should
Be here. At eleven twenty-nine we're to have
The total eclipse of the sun, to which I've invited them.
The mouth of the moon has already begun to munch.
We shall all feel ourselves making a north-west passage
Through the sea of heaven, and darkness will cover
The face of the earth. In that moment
All women will be as one.

EDGAR.   That's what I was going
To ask you. I don't want to play the heavy son,
But would you say you loved these women equally?

DUKE. Equality is a mortuary word. Just choose.
Shall I be happy on Tuesdays, Thursdays, and Saturdays,
Or on Mondays, Wednesdays, and Fridays? Some such difference
Is all that your choice involves.

Enter CAPTAIN FOX REDDLEMAN, *a manservant. He looks like,
and was once, a lion tamer.*

REDDLEMAN.   'Scuse, your Grace:
But a telegram for our little friend Mr. Reedbeck.

A telegram, Mr. Reedbeck. B'Jason, four
Flights I've had to come up to bring it to you.
Please Jenny it's worth it. And the boy's waiting.

EDGAR. Well, father, I don't know; with a certain sense
Of preconceiving myself, I may come back.
I shall do what I can for you; I only hope
You'll not live to regret the way my fancy
Takes you.

[*Exit* EDGAR.

REEDBECK.   Oh! Would you ever think
Such a joy could happen to me, in the world as we know it?

REDDLEMAN. I have to tell your Grace, in all decency
To the footman Bates, who I religiously despise,
If the fellow comes on duty with a bloody nose
'Tis my doing, and long may it bleed. And h'wot
About the boy below, Mr. Reedbeck? Any answer?

REEDBECK. No, no, Reddleman, only thanksgiving.
Oh, and I suppose a shilling, he'd like a shilling.

DUKE. And go gently with Bates, Reddleman, or else
You'll drive him back to his old nervous habits
Of biting his nails and burglary. Remember
You're not a lion tamer now.

REDDLEMAN.   And that
Was a hit below—I'm wearing no belt—below
The navel. Thank God I'm severed from my mother
Or she would have felt it severely. I'd remind you
'Twas fighting for king and country I lost me nerve.
And b'Daniel, it's a sad job to be parted
From the lords of the jungle.

DUKE.   I'm sorry, Reddleman;
I wasn't meaning to hurt you.

REDDLEMAN.   Well, go easy,
Go easy with me, your Grace. Now, Mr. Reedbeck:
Thanksgiving and a bob for the boy below:
Very good.

                                        [*Exit* REDDLEMAN.

REEDBECK. A red-letter day for me, your Grace;
Let me see: the twenty-ninth of October?

DUKE.   Yes;
The leaves transfigured by the thought of death,
The wind south-west, a blue sky buffaloed
By cloud, the sun approaching its eclipse.

REEDBECK. You remember I have a daughter? I've spoken of her
From time to time; I had the astounding fortune
To beget her, as though I'd been chosen to release
A rose from the world's rock; and then I had
The misery to lose her, when her mother
Left me for America, ten years ago.
Well, now I'm holding in my hand a message
Which says she's returning to me, returning to-day,
No time of arrival, just bare and astonishing
'Am in England hope to kiss you before lunch
Perpetua.' I can hardly believe it could happen,
I can't believe so, not in the world as we know it.

DUKE. Go easy, Reedbeck, go easy with yourself.

REEDBECK. If she should come in time for the eclipse——

DUKE. Then, of course, she shall join us to see the eclipse.
It will be a change for her after America.
I'm going now, to dress. Subdue yourself, Reedbeck.
Otherwise you'll capsize in disappointment.
Expect the worst.

                                        [*Exit the* DUKE.

REEDBECK.   Not at all, oh, no, not at all,
No shadows of that sort.
                                   [*He hums to the telephone.*
                         Must warn my housekeeper.
'I galloped, Dirck galloped, we galloped all three . . .'
Oh, Mrs. Lendy, Mr. Reedbeck here; I have to ask you
To prepare a room for my daughter. I'm so glad
To hear you gasp. However, we must keep our heads,
Such as they are. Tell her to join us here
And ask to be shown to the Observatory Room.
There will be refreshment for her, and a total
Eclipse of the sun.
                  Enter DOMINIC, REEDBECK'S *son.*

DOMINIC.   I want to speak to you.
How long are we likely to be alone?

REEDBECK.   In a moment,
Dominic dear. You'll put her some flowers, Mrs. Lendy.
Are the Helianthus gone? Well, *uliginosum.*
You call them chrysanthemums, I think. And on her bed
The lilac linen sheets. Some time before lunch.
Good-bye. Oh, Dominic, my dear, dear boy,
Your sister's coming home!

DOMINIC [*silent, and then*].   That makes you happy.

REEDBECK. Oh, dear, it's one of your knock-the-bottom-
Out-of-everything mornings. Or do you mean
You've heard, and you know what's bringing her home?
I hope nothing's amiss?

DOMINIC.   Not with her.

REEDBECK.   Well, then——

DOMINIC. Do I say what I have to say *here*? Or do we go back
To the house? It isn't going to be pleasant.

REEDBECK.   Of course it is.
There's nothing unpleasant that isn't going to be pleasant.
Perpetua's returning to me; the world
Is no longer depressed at the poles, and everything
Will be pleasant: the east wind, smoking fires,
Revolution, debility——

DOMINIC.   Jail?

REEDBECK.   Yes, jail,
Solitary confinement, the cat-o'-nine-tails,
Your Aunt Florence——

DOMINIC.   Can you keep your feet
On sober earth for five difficult minutes
And talk responsibly? Why are we so rich?
I've asked you before; but you, a Duke's bailiff,
An agent: where did our money come from?

REEDBECK. Have you no capacity for delight?
Do for all our sakes be pleasant, dear boy.

DOMINIC. You said our money came from legacies, you told me
From legacies!

REEDBECK.   Just so; we've been very fortunate.
Your Uncle Hector, when he put on immortality
In Tasmania, increased, to a certain extent,
Our freedom from care; and old Lady Bright, my first
Employer, when she passed on, passed on
Herself to heaven and the rest to me; and then——

DOMINIC. I have to ask for figures. My Uncle Hector
Died, leaving——?

REEDBECK.   Don't let's talk of death.
I've a heart this morning as light as a nebula.
But you, you sombre boy, you can't even

F

Sputter up a few sparks when I tell you
Your sister's coming home!

DOMINIC.   Died, leaving——?

REEDBECK.   Really,
How can I be expected to remember?
There was some music, certainly; the piano score
Of *The Quaker Girl*; and I recollect some ninepins;
And a small South American lizard called Faithful
Which died in quarantine. But Lady Bright——

DOMINIC. You've stolen the money, haven't you: steadily
And consistently? O God, why ask? I know
Already. And thieved with so little subtlety
Anyone might know. Raised rents
But entered in your books at the old figure;
Sale of produce and timber, at prices higher
Than you've recorded. I've been ferreting,
Ever since an unmistakable innuendo
From Bates the footman.

REEDBECK.   Come now; Bates
Is a common burglar, and sees, of course,
His reflection in all about him. He was caught
Red-handed with the silver, and his Grace,
Being short of staff at the time, asked him to stay
And clean it.

DOMINIC.   Bates is quite a decent fellow.
I've had a long talk to him. He used to suffer
From a pathological lust for climbing ladders
And had to rationalize it when he got
To the top. And now he's determined to be honest,
Even if it makes him ill, he says. But with you
It's unrelieved, wicked cupidity.
Of course I go down from Cambridge. I couldn't stay there

When any morning I might wake up and find
I'd become the son of a convict. We're both in
For misery now, and Perpetua comes home
Just in time to share it.

REEDBECK.   I wish I could explain
How very mistaken I'm sure you must be. Especially
On such a cheerful morning. It's really too bad.
We have the dark every twelve hours as it is
Without inventing more.

Enter BATES: *he shows a trace of rough handling. He announces* MISS
ROSABEL FLEMING, *and withdraws.*

ROSABEL. I expected to find the Duke here.

REEDBECK.   The competitors!
I'd forgotten them. You'll forgive me, madam, I hope;
You find me a little disjunct. His Grace
Will join us shortly. My name is Reedbeck.
This was my son.

ROSABEL.   Was your son?

REEDBECK.   There's no
Other tense for me now except the past,
Miss Belmont. You were Miss Belmont?

ROSABEL.   Rosabel Fleming.
I am still Rosabel Fleming.

DOMINIC.   Please excuse me.
I'd like to know you, but I can't look anyone
Happily in the eye. I'm pleased to have met you.

                                        [*Exit* DOMINIC.
ROSABEL. Is he in trouble?

REEDBECK.   The paradoxes of virtue
Have confused him. Won't you sit down, Miss Fleming?

ROSABEL. I begin to understand why the theatre
Gives me so little work.
That could scarcely have been called a splendid entrance,
Even by the most loving.

REEDBECK.   Go down from Cambridge.
Did you hear him say that? No, you were not here.
It let all the life out of me for a moment.
All the Latin I have myself, you know,
Is horticultural: *muscari comosum*
Monstrosum, and *scrophularia nodosa*,
Et cetera ad infinitum. But how I longed
As a boy for the groves and grooves of Academe.
Give me civilization, Miss Fleming; you can keep
Your progress.

ROSABEL.   This room, surely, is something new?

REEDBECK. The Observatory Room, giving upon
An uninterrupted sweep of the Surrey heavens;
At night the weeping stars; by day——

                    Enter MRS. JESSIE DILL.

JESSIE.   I'm sorry.
I thought it would be just his Grace. I'll go again.

REEDBECK. No, no, his Grace will be here. By day
The brandishing sun inciting the earth
To revolution and rotation——

JESSIE.   I'm Mrs. Dill.
It's my own fault the man hasn't announced me.
It seemed to me 'All those stairs, for the poor young chap
Just to say Here's Jessie.' He went on insisting,
Of course, but when we got to the second landing
He must have thought it was getting a bit undignified
Both of us coming up two steps at a time.

So he slid back down the banisters.
Surely I've met you before, dear?

ROSABEL.   Rosabel Fleming.

JESSIE. I should have remembered. I saw you, once upon a time,
Being very sweet in a play about Ophelia.
And this is a strange thing, too, being up here
In this room together. You'd hardly recognize it.
Well, I don't know, I should say that's a telescope.

ROSABEL. I think I must go. I hadn't understood
The Duke would have visitors. . . .

REEDBECK.   We were just talking
About this room when you came, Mrs. Dill. My name
Is Reedbeck. This was one of his Grace's
Bedrooms, as perhaps. . . . But now, as you see,
He prefers to regard the skies here, scavenging
Through the night for knowledge. He also uses
The room for experiments.

JESSIE.   He always did.

ROSABEL. I've decided not to stay. I only came in
For a moment, finding myself not far away.
If you'd be kind enough to tell him——

Enter the DUKE.

DUKE.   Good morning, Rosabel.
Good morning, Jessie.

JESSIE.   Here he is, himself.
He's the same boy, God bless him, not a day older,
Even if he does have to use a telescope.

DUKE. Flattery, Jessie; for years the frost has lain
On my stubble beard. The swallows and other such
Migratory birds have left me months ago.

JESSIE. You must build yourself a nice fire.

DUKE.   No, Jessie;
I have to consider my years and decline with the sun,
Gracefully but gratefully decline.
I have also to apologize for keeping you waiting.
I was up all night with the universe again
And slept late. Or is that not to be
Forgiven? A silence broods on Rosabel.

ROSABEL. I was conscious of it. I was wondering
What note to sound. I'm suddenly very uncertain
Why I'm here.

DUKE.   For a total eclipse of the sun.
Didn't I mention it to you in my letter?

ROSABEL. Is there some tradition that old friends should meet
again
During an eclipse? Or what other reason? Your birthday?
No, you're a Sagittarian. This is only October.

DUKE. And the leaves are falling. What shall a robin do then,
Poor thing?

JESSIE.   Sit in this barn, and keep himself warm,
And tuck himself up alone in the east wing,
Poor thing.

Enter EDGAR.

DUKE.   My son Edgar, Miss Rosabel Fleming.
I introduce Rosabel first, Jessie, to give you
Time to enjoy your joke. My son Edgar,
Mrs. Dill.

JESSIE.   How lovely it is to meet you.
I've known your father, you know, ever since
I was ever so slim. Though, of course, properly speaking,
It was my husband who was really his friend.

Please return to:-

County Reserve Store
Malling Brooks

CL 512

I hope your father will allow me to say
His friend.

DUKE.   I'm delighted to let you say it.
I didn't know he had ever been alive
Or we might have said it before.

EDGAR.   It's just as well
We understand my father.

ROSABEL.   And it's just as well
We don't all have to. It's a thing I have no love for,
To have to go groping along the corridors
Of someone else's mind, so that I shan't
Be hurt. No one has any right to ask it.

DUKE. We're not, I hope, in this mellow October light
Getting ill at ease? We're here this morning to watch
The sun annulled and renewed, and to sit affectionately
Over the year's dilapidation. 'Mellow'
Is the keynote of the hour. We must be mellow,
Remembering we've been on the earth two million years,
Man and boy and Sterkfontein ape.

REEDBECK [*singing abstractedly at the window*].
                        You call me old
                        But I am still
            A chippy young chap on Chipperton Hill
                        And shall be, while
                        My flesh can cover
            The bones of a bona-fide lover.
            Heydilly, heydilly, hang me a sheep.

DUKE. Happy, happy Reedbeck. He has a daughter
Returning to him.

JESSIE.   And there he sits and purrs
As though the morning was a saucer of milk.

REEDBECK. I caught myself singing. I do beg your pardon.

EDGAR. Sing away, Reedbeck. Bring her in with music.
This is wonderful news.

[BATES *at the door*.

REEDBECK. Can this be—is it . . .?

[BATES *announces, and enter*, MRS. TAYLOR-SNELL.

DUKE. The exact Hilda. Punctuality
Was drawing its last breath. The sun has mooned
Away half its light already.

HILDA. A party, Hereward?
You didn't tell me.

DUKE. I scarcely knew. And anyway
We shall all feel quite alone, except, perhaps, Jessie.
Mrs. Dill, Mrs. Taylor-Snell. There will only be
The appearance of people being near to us.
Miss Rosabel Fleming, Mrs. Taylor-Snell.
Reedbeck you know. You've disappointed him..
He hoped you would have been his daughter.

HILDA. Did you ever propose it, Reedbeck?

REEDBECK. You see before you
A creaking bough on which, at any moment,
A dear young daughter may alight.

DUKE. My extension in time: Edgar.

EDGAR. Five feet ten
Of my unlimited father.

HILDA. I have often
Expected to meet you.

EDGAR. I suppose so;
But until he's dead I'm really a redundancy.
I make him feel bifurcated.

JESSIE.   Wherever
Does he learn those terrible words?

EDGAR.   I spend
Such a lot of my time in the stables.

DUKE [*to* BATES, *who has loitered by the door*]. What is it, Bates?

BATES.   There are faces
As can be mauled about wiv, and there are faces
As can't be mauled about wiv. Mine can't
Be mauled about wiv. Memo, guvnor, to be 'anded
On to the proper quarters, and *you* know
What basket I refers to.
Will that be all, guvnor?

DUKE.   That will be all, Bates.

      [*Exit* BATES. REEDBECK *throws open the window and leans
      out.*

HILDA. Be careful, Reedbeck! There really is such a thing
As the force of gravity.

REEDBECK.   Only the wind blowing
And the rattle of leaves. I hoped it would prove to be
Internal combustion.

DUKE [*aside to* EDGAR]. I should have mentioned to you,
The case of Athene is minutely complicated
By a husband. But don't be deflected. He would still
Have the shooting over the estate. Nothing
Is insurmountable.

EDGAR.   Except yourself,
I take you to mean. But it's all right;
I'm devoted to you.

HILDA.   Why don't you give it up,
Reedbeck? There's no daughter there. How much
This house has aged, Hereward, since I saw it

Last. I was thinking so coming up the stairs.
It looks as though the walls have cried themselves
To sleep for nights on end. And the number of windows
Broken! I don't think you should throw nearly
So many stones. The spiders are larger, the jackdaws
Ruder, the servants more eccentric. You mustn't
Drift into Gothic, when your physique is so
Stubbornly Norman.

DUKE.   I see no point in trying
To make time look as though it were standing still
By renewing the face of it. I like to watch my own
Deft and reckless plunge into ancient history.
It assuages my lust for speed. Dark glasses for the ladies,
Reedbeck; tell them to look at the sun.

EDGAR.   And to pray
For all small birds under the eye of the hawk.

JESSIE. I can remember, when I was a kid,
Being got out of bed and told I had to look
At something in the sky. I kept on saying
Oh, yes, mum, isn't it lovely, isn't it lovely?
It was a comet or a zeppelin or something,
But all I could see was the usual end
Of the Crystal Palace.

REEDBECK [*handing glasses*]. Look at the sun, Mrs. Dill.

JESSIE. And now I can't help feeling
As if I'd just been got out of bed again
To look at something I probably shan't see.

DUKE. That's the human predicament, in a nutshell.

ROSABEL. There's a kind of humour abroad this morning that
    seems to
Put me outside the party.

REEDBECK. Look at the sun, Miss Fleming.

ROSABEL. Thank you.

EDGAR. I've such a feeling of pre-natal
Tension, it's more than a boy can bear. Father,
I'm going to make the decision now
And pin the future down for you.

HILDA. But will you
Find that easy? I couldn't help overhearing.
The future has the most uncertain temper.
After all you've said, Hereward, do you teach
Your child to tamper with time?

DUKE. He had it to play with
When he was young; but he'll soon see
How it will rag him to death. Meanwhile, the eclipse.
Let me be your guide. Observe how Sol Salome
Almost hidden by the head of the Baptist moon
Dances her last few steps of fire.

HILDA. You're confusing
The sex of the sun.

DUKE. It's the act itself: observe
The copulation of Jove, magnificent in
Mid air.

JESSIE. The bulk of the moon, creeping on
And on. It makes me feel more solemn than I've ever
Felt before at eleven o'clock in the morning.

EDGAR. No nice eclipse for you, Miss Fleming?

ROSABEL. Why, yes,
It was what your father invited me to see.
I was far away for the moment.

EDGAR.   Before you go
To the window, I wonder if you'd mind accepting this apple?

ROSABEL. No, thank you. I'll go and see what there is to be seen
Before it's too late.

EDGAR.   Father, may I have your attention?
There, Miss Fleming, it will come in useful sometime.

DUKE. Daylight, you see, is shamming twilight. Nature
Is being made a fool of. Three or four stars, there,
You can see them wince, where only a moment earlier
Morning was all serene. The crows, with much
Misgiving, talk themselves into their trees. Even
The usually phlegmatic owls
Care a hoot or two. The bats from the barn
Make one flickering flight, and return to hang
Their heads. All of them tricked and fuddled
By the passing of a small cadaverous planet.

HILDA. Yes, we understand the event perfectly.

JESSIE. Let him enjoy it. Space, ever and ever,
On and on. . . . Well, I don't know.

EDGAR. Father, I don't know whether you have noticed:
A certain event has occurred.

DUKE.   Is now occurring.
We're crossing perceptibly into the dark.
Daylight differences are made subordinate
To the general shade.

EDGAR.   Father, for God's sake, look!
I am giving Miss Fleming an apple.

ROSABEL.   You've already
Given me an apple.

DUKE.   I observe you're plying

Rosabel with fruit. *Bis dat qui cito dat.*
We can now turn our attention again to the sun.

EDGAR. So a revolutionary change begins
Without raising a hand's turn of the dust.
Ah, well; give me some dark glass.

HILDA.   What a shame
If that cloud spoils the climax for us.

REEDBECK.   No,
It avoids, you see; it glides mercifully
And dexterously past. I hope and pray
The same will be true of the cloud that hangs over my own
Sunshine: but young men can be so ruthless,
So ruthless; it's terrible to think about.

DUKE. What now, Reedbeck?

REEDBECK.   Ah, yes; to the cosmos it doesn't
Matter; I suppose I agree.

JESSIE.   To think
We're in the shadow of old Lunabella.

DUKE.   To think.

JESSIE. When she moves over will she see us
Coming out of her shadow? Are we really
As bright as a moon, from the moon's side of the question?

DUKE. We have a borrowed brilliance. At night
Among the knots and clusters and corner boys
Of the sky, among asteroids and cepheids,
With Sirius, Mercury, and Canis Major,
Among nebulae and magellanic cloud,
You shine, Jessie.

JESSIE.   You're making me self-conscious.

DUKE. Here we're as dull as unwashed plates; out there
       We shine. That's a consideration. Come
       Close to paradise, and where's the lustre?
       But still, at some remove, we shine, and truth
       We hope is content to keep a distant prospect.
       So you, Jessie, and the swamps of the equator,
       Shine; the boring overplus of ocean,
       The Walworth Road, the Parthenon, and Reedbeck
       Shine; the dark tree with the nightingale
       At heart, dockyards, the desert, the newly dead,
       Minarets, gasometers, and even I
       Fall into space in one not unattractive
       Beam. To take us separately is to stare
       At mud; only together, at long range,
       We coalesce in light.

JESSIE.   I like to think I'm being
       A ray of light to some nice young couple out there.
       'There's the Great Bear,' they'd say, and 'Look,
       There's old Jessie, tilted on her side
       Just over the Charing Cross Hotel.'

HILDA.   You both
       Chatter so. It's a moment for quiet. Who knows
       If ever I'll see this again.

EDGAR.   The end of our lord
       The sun.

ROSABEL. It's no good. I must get out into the air!
       It's impossible to breathe up here!

DUKE.   What is it,
       Rosabel? Claustrophobia on the brink
       Of the free heavens? Come now, think of it
       As the usual dipping of day's flag. You used
       To love this room at night.

ROSABEL. How do you know?
How can you tell who loves, or when or why they love,
You without a single beat of heart
Worth measuring? You sit up here all night
Looking at the stars, travelling farther and farther
Away from living people. I hate your telescope!
How can you know, and what, if you knew, can it mean,
What can the darkest bruise on the human mind
Mean, when nothing beats against you heavier
Than a fall of rain? And out you whip
Your impervious umbrella of satisfaction!
How you prink across every puddle, and laugh
To think that other men can drown.
You would never believe there are some affections
Which would rather have decent burial
Than this mocking perpetuation you offer them.
You're a devil, a devil, a devil, a devil!

DUKE. Only
On one side of the family, Rosabel,
Please believe that.

EDGAR [*taking the apple from her hand*].
I beg your pardon; I think
I've made a mistake.

ROSABEL. Now I must go. I've spoilt
The eclipse. For that I'm sorry.

DUKE. It's frankly impossible
To spoil the eclipse.

REEDBECK. It would be fanciful
No doubt to say that the moon has placed a penny
Not on the dead but on the living eye of the sun.

EDGAR. Yes, Reedbeck, it would.

JESSIE.   Don't you be put down.
It's nice that anyone can say anything at all.

DUKE. So Rosabel believes when the cold spell comes
And we're compelled to enter this draughty time
And shuffle about in the slipshod leaves,
Leaves disbanded, leaves at a loose end,
And we know we're in for the drifting of the fall,
We should merely shiver and be silent: never speak
Of the climate of Eden, or the really magnificent
Foliage of the tree of knowledge,
Or the unforgettable hushed emerald
Of the coiling and fettering serpent:
Pretend we never knew it, because love
Quite naturally condescended
To the passing of time. But why should we, Rosabel?

HILDA. But if what I gather to be true is true,
Though it's no business of mine,
I must say, Hereward, you certainly seem to have been
Coruscating on thin ice. I think
She has cause to be angry. I do think so.
You've behaved a great deal less than well.

DUKE. I've behaved according to my lights of love
Which were excellent and bright and much to be
Remembered. You have all of you been my moments
Of revelation. I wish I understood why
You want to behave like skeletons in my cupboard.

JESSIE. Not Jessie, alas; her weight is all against it.
But need we make Miss Fleming cry?

EDGAR.   I'd like it,
Father, if Mrs. Dill would have this apple.

JESSIE. I'd like it, too; though it's prettier on the tree.

ROSABEL. Your moments of revelation! I only wonder
What we revealed. Certainly not
What goes on in other hearts than your own.
That's as remote to you as a seaside lodging-house
To a passing whale.

HILDA.   Could she put it more fairly?

JESSIE. I remember seeing what was thought to be a whale
At somewhere like Tenby; at least, my father said
Look, there's a whale, Jessie; but all I saw
Was the tip of a fin which might have been finnan haddy
Or Father Neptune or an old forgotten
Channel swimmer.

REEDBECK.   Can you play with Leviathan
As with a bird? That's really quite the strangest
Of rhetorical questions. And when will my daughter come?

DUKE. Rosabel——

JESSIE.   We might as well never have changed the subject.

DUKE. Rosabel, why pick on me to be
The villain? I'm a Roman in a world
Of Romans, and all creation can recognize me
As genus Man. Old men, young men, virgins,
Viragoes, all walk hand in hand with me
In the green enclosure of insensibility.
An individual torment in Indo-China
Makes less noise in your ear than the drop of a fir cone.
So why do I have to be sensible
Of a heart which is fortunate enough to be
Four thousand miles nearer my way, someone,
Moreover, to whom I've already given pleasure
And the refuge of a bed, which I never gave
(Such is my frailty) to the Indo-Chinee?

Don't let's go mad with inconsistency.
Either everything shall be near, or everything
Shall be far. Allow me the wrong end of the telescope;
I like to conform.

JESSIE.   Mr. Reedbeck will propose
The vote of thanks.

REEDBECK.   I really think, a few moments ago,
I heard what could only have been a motor-car.

ROSABEL. Where have I got myself now? Into such
An embarrassment, if I could vanish I should vanish,
And even then transparently kick myself.
It was hopelessly stupid.

HILDA.   Stupid, and what was called,
In the days when musk had a scent, indelicate.

DUKE. I shall plough up the orchard, Edgar;
It was never a great success.

              [*The shadow lifts from the sun, and the light falls on*
              PERPETUA REEDBECK.

EDGAR.   God be praised,
The sun again.

REEDBECK.   My daughter, it's my daughter, Perpetua,
My dear, my dear!

                                        [PERPETUA *runs to him.*

ROSABEL.   Where shall I hide a most
Unhappy head?

                                        [*Exit* ROSABEL.

REEDBECK.   O my little sixpenny
Ha'penny daughter, home again, home again,
Home again!

HILDA [*thinking of* ROSABEL].
      Can she take care of herself, that woman?
             [*She follows* ROSABEL.

PERPETUA. Let me look at you. Every feature where I left it
Ten years ago! I'd forgotten you were so beautiful.

REEDBECK. You mustn't spoil me, not so soon;
I shall puff myself up and explode like a frog.

PERPETUA. Perhaps we should sing until we're used to it?
Might that be the wise thing?

REEDBECK.   I should stop at every
Note to listen to you. But, my dear,
I must present you to his Grace. I'd forgotten
We were not in heaven. Your Grace—this—
This is——

DUKE.   Steady, Reedbeck.
Let me dry your eyes. Dear man, these tears are something
Remarkably like champagne.

REEDBECK.   No doubt they are.
My dear daughter: his Grace the Duke of Altair.

DUKE. You have made your father as happy as if his heart
Were breaking. And isn't it likely you're going to make
Others happy as well? We have only autumn
To offer you, England's moist and misty devotion,
But spring may come in time to reconcile you
If you'll wait so long.

PERPETUA.   I need no reconciling.
I was born and grew in this green and pleasant aquarium,
And I've spent four days on a wicked October sea
For love of recollected mildew
And my dear frog-father; only I'd scarcely expected
Quite so much impenetrable murk

In the middle of morning. Surely there must be something
Out of sorts about your daylight?

DUKE.   Nothing
Which time won't mend. But, first, let me introduce—
Ah, they've left us; Hilda and Rosabel
Have passed away with no last word. They always
Bore themselves with the true brevity of empires.
But here is Mrs. Dill, more universe
Than empire, less conquered but more embracing.

JESSIE. I'm very pleased to meet you. Your father loves you
With every word in the language.

DUKE.   And this, Miss Reedbeck,
Is my first youth, my younger days: The Marquis
Of Charlock.

EDGAR.   You're a kind of legend with us here,
But the truth is better.

PERPETUA.   I'll tell you the truth:
I'm very happy this morning; I'm really out
Of prison.

REEDBECK.   Of prison, my darling? Why do you say
Of prison?

PERPETUA.   I mean, of course, the boat was a prison
And the frowning sea was Dartmoor.

DUKE.   To refresh you
There's wine in the bottle, cider from the wood,
Biscuits in the barrel; and there you can see
Our English sun, convalescent after passing
Through the valley of the shadow of the moon.

PERPETUA. So that was why I had to search my way
Up the stairs in gloom. How far off is the sun?

DUKE. The best part of ninety-three million miles.

PERPETUA. You would hardly think it could matter.

EDGAR. What will you
    drink,
  Miss Reedbeck?

PERPETUA. Something of England, the cider, presently.
  I'm so at peace, though I still can feel
  The lunge of the sea. Your floor isn't meant to sway?

DUKE. The floor is battering at your feet like Attila
  With a horde of corybantic atoms,
  And travelling at eighteen miles a second,
  But it cannot be said to sway.

JESSIE. That would be much
  Too easy.

DUKE. Our stability is a matter
  For surprise.

REEDBECK. I feel the terrible truth of that.
  Even now, for example, when I see my Perpetua
  Sitting like a girl on a swing on an Easter Monday
  Under a Wedgwood sky, I can feel my heart——

PERPETUA. That's just what it's like, a girl on a swing.

REEDBECK. My heart
  Knocking most anxiously against the future,
  As though afraid to be alone with the present time:
  Ready, really, for almost any disaster
  Rather than this unsteady tight-rope of joy
  I'm walking on now. Are you ill, perhaps? Is that it?
  Have you come home for your health?

PERPETUA. I've come home to be home.
  A pigeon's return—just so simple, Poppadillo.

I wanted to stand where I first grew, and to have
My roots and my branches all in one place together.
And that's no curious thing. Here, swinging
On my swing, with the Atlantic foam still racing
Under my eyelids, I seem at rest already.
And so I sent no word to say I was coming,
Because, in the sense that means the most,
I was here all the time.

EDGAR.   And so you emerged
Like Venus from the sea.

PERPETUA.   But sicker.

REEDBECK.   What
Shall I do for my returning Mayflower
Suppose she is disappointed in the land
Her roots are in?

PERPETUA.   You needn't be afraid.
If this is still an island
Enclosed in a druid circle of stony sea,
As misty as it was that chilly Thursday
When I was born to the wilting of plovers
And the smell of a saturation of hops,
Then I'm safely and happily home.

JESSIE.   Here's to your happiness,
Dear; God save the King, and a mild winter.

REEDBECK. Your happiness, my dear.

EDGAR.   Happiness, Miss Reedbeck.

DUKE. I should like you to offer Miss Reedbeck an apple, Edgar.

EDGAR. Anything except an apple, father.
I will offer her
The cloudy peach, the bristling pineapple,

The dropsical pear, the sportive orange,
Apricot, sloe, King William, or a carillon
Of grapes, but not, as God's my judge, an apple.

DUKE. Then, as Paris abdicates, I must offer
The sweet round robin fruit myself—

> [*He holds an apple up between his fingers.*

The green sphere the myth of the world began in,
Which Melanion let fall, delaying
Mercurial Atalanta—

> [PERPETUA *has whipped a very small pistol from a pig-skin
> holster at her belt. She shoots and shatters the apple. There
> is an incredulous, shaken silence.*

PERPETUA. I—I'm terribly sorry. That was thoughtless of me.
Perhaps you wanted to eat it.

DUKE.   There are others;
Nature is pleased to give us more. And you
Have been very good; you let me keep my fingers.

REEDBECK. Only by the mercy of God! My dear girl,
My dear girl! What in the world possessed you?
You might have been the death of him!

PERPETUA.   No, it was quite safe.
To please, I always aim. But that, I agree,
Is no excuse. It was dreadful, and shameful of me.
I was thinking of something else, or else
It would never have happened.

> *Enter* ROSABEL, *followed by* HILDA.

ROSABEL.   What was it? We heard a sound
Like a shot!

REEDBECK.   Good gracious, a *sound* like a shot!

HILDA. Is no one hurt?

DUKE.   An apple came to grief
As apples must.

EDGAR.   One pip too many.

JESSIE.   And nobody
Was more surprised than the Duke.

REEDBECK.   Oh, yes, I think so,
I think my surprise can hardly have been bettered
Except, no doubt, by the apple. And I'm still
Anchored in amazement, I have to confess.

PERPETUA. I also have to confess; I see I must.
I thought I could come back again to England
And slip into this new beginning, silently.
But now the pistol has gone off; the silence anyway
Is well and truly broken, and so I'll explain,
Though the explanation, I'm afraid, will seem
As wild as the shot.

REEDBECK.   What can it be? Be quick
And tell me.

PERPETUA.   I've lately been in prison. But not
For what we should call a crime.

REEDBECK.   They put you in prison
Without rhyme or reason?

PERPETUA.   There may have been
A little rhyme. I was thought to be unsafe
For democracy, because I broke, or shot,
Or burnt, a good many things, or rather—and this
Is the reason—a bad many things: the unsightly,
The gimcrack, the tedious, the hideous, the spurious,
The harmful. Not I alone, of course;
We were all students, and called ourselves

The Society for the Desecration
Of Ancient and Modern Monumental Errors.
We destroyed, or tried to destroy, whatever we loathed
As bad.

ROSABEL. Whatever you loathed, you destroyed?
Why, that was admirable, superb, the most
Heavenly daring!

PERPETUA.   No, I think it was only
Exasperation. And then we went to prison.
And there I knew it was all no use.
The more we destroyed, the worse the bad sprang up.
And I thought and thought, What can I do for the world?
I was wearing the prison drab. My name was a number.
Inside or outside the prison, Perpetua
(I thought), you're no one, you're everybody's colour.
You must make good, before you break the bad,
Perpetua. And so I came home to England
Simply to trace myself, in my own way.

                    [*She offers the pistol to the* DUKE.

I'd better surrender this. I only kept it
For a kind of memento. And I apologize
Again for destroying the apple. Still half at sea
As I am, it appeared to be, in a misty way,
Like a threat to my new-come freedom.

DUKE. I hope you will think so again, some other time.

ROSABEL [*taking the pistol*]. May I have it, to remind me of your
    story,
To know there has been someone in the world
Who dared to do such things! If only I
Could be such a brave one, there might be
Some justification for me.

DUKE [*taking it from her*].   Caps for you,
Dear Rosabel, not bullets. I'll have it
Filled for your next big scene.

> [*A gong booms from below.*

EDGAR. Luncheon! Can we be supposed to eat
On a day when the sun is drowned by the moon,
And apples meet such a strange end?

DUKE. I see nothing strange. If we can move and talk
Under the sun at all, we must have accepted
The incredible as commonplace, long ago;
And even the incredible must eat.
Shall we go down?

THE CURTAIN FALLS ON ACT ONE

ACT TWO

SCENE ONE

The Temple of the Ancient Virtues, beside the ducal lake, in the after-noon. DOMINIC *and* PERPETUA *are there.*

DOMINIC. You haven't spoken for three and a half minutes.

———————

    Four minutes. This is the most pregnant pause
    Since darkness was on the face of the deep. I suppose
    You think I shouldn't have told you.

PERPETUA.   Oh, yes, you should.

DOMINIC. It was better than leaving you in a fool's paradise,
    You must admit.

PERPETUA.   I could be twice as silent
    For seven times as long.

DOMINIC.   Well, then you shall be.
    I know myself how the shock stuns one.

PERPETUA.   No shock
    At all. I was able to believe you at once.
    Poppadillo has the most beguiling
    Jackdaw look about him. But you think
    He wouldn't be happy in prison?

DOMINIC.   He wouldn't, but what
    Difference does that make? Would you be able
    To look anyone in the face, with a father jailed?

PERPETUA. Oh, yes, if he were comfortable. But I think
He might feel shut in. No, Dominic, I'm sure
You're right. If someone has to go to prison,
I must.

DOMINIC. You? What can you possibly mean?

PERPETUA. You said I should have to, and now all I mean
Is Yes, quite so.

DOMINIC.   Quite what is quite so, will you tell me?

PERPETUA. I heard you say, perhaps it might have been
Six minutes ago, if I made myself agreeable
The Duke (you said) being much in that mind at the moment
Might, with any luck, be inclined to marry me,
And no gentleman (you added) would incriminate
His father-in-law. And I agree with you,
And I see my carefree hours already numbered,
My freedom of choice and my individual day.
I'm no longer a woman after my own heart.
Broad cupid's arrows on my wedding veil.
But still, Dominic, for my father's sake
Not ours, I mean to try.

DOMINIC.   God bless you, then,
And God speed you, and thank God I can breathe again.
And a coronet's no martyrdom, particularly
When it sits on a man whom women find easy to like.

PERPETUA. I wonder how many women have stood perplexed
And plagued in this temple, two whole centuries of them,
Looking out this way, on the same view
Of the metal rusting year. Lemon, amber,
Umber, bronze and brass, oxblood, damson,
Crimson, scalding scarlet, black cedar,
And the willow's yellow fall to grace.

DOMINIC. Do you have to be so melancholy? Everything
   Is better now. Though there is still the anxiety
   Whether you can prepossess him before he strikes.

PERPETUA. Oh, yes, there is that anxiety still.
   Here comes the straying lamb who gave us life.

DOMINIC. Don't pamper him. We have to make him realize
   He's been sinning all this while.

PERPETUA.   He looks as worried
   As though he knew it already.

           Enter REEDBECK, *out of breath.*

REEDBECK.   So here—here—
   You are. I wondered, missed you, but luckily caught
   Sight of you going down through the trees. I lost
   My hat on the way; it blew (oh, what a gasping old fellow)
   Off, blew off; now upside down on the water
   Among the *Alisma Plantago-aquatica.*
   Didn't think I should have enough breath to say so.

PERPETUA. Try only breathing, for a time; that's always
   Nice.

DOMINIC. What was the hurry? Did you think I was going
   To throw her in the water?

REEDBECK.   Among the *Alisma*
   Plantago-aquatica. Has he been talking to you?
   He's not as fond of me as either of us
   Would like.

PERPETUA.   I've been hearing unimaginable
   Things about you.

REEDBECK.   Yes, the imagination
   Is a frail craft, soon capsizes, quite understand.
   Now this, my dear, called sometimes the Temple
   Of the Ancient Virtues, and at other times

The White Temple, both because it is white
And because it was designed by Martin White
In seventeen hundred and ninety-three, was erected
By the third Duke of Altair for his wife Claire
For her use when she played the part of the Delphic Oracle,
A way she had of informing the Duke of her pregnancy,
Which she did on twenty-seven separate occasions.

PERPETUA. Tell me why you've been cheating the Duke,
There's a good boy. What made you do it?

REEDBECK.   I hope
I've done nothing so monosyllabic as to cheat.
A spade is never so merely a spade as the word
Spade would imply.

DOMINIC.   One's helpless to help him.

PERPETUA. Poppadillo, suppose I put it this way:
What made you supercherify with chousery
The Duke?

REEDBECK.   That might be said to—that perhaps
Is not an unfair expression. And I say in reply
The reason was the fading charm of the world.
The banquet of civilization is over——

PERPETUA.   Shall we call it
The groaning board?

REEDBECK.   You may call it what you will.
With a little wealth to do it I should like to perform
The grace after the meat, a last, gentlemanly,
Valedictory grace: a grace for departing grace
(Is that not rather good?):
The spacious lawns of life are being
Inevitably ploughed, and we don't know, we really
Don't know, what's going to be sown there.

Dignity has dropped upon all fours.
Indeed there's hardly to be seen
One intense perpendicular
In all the streets of men. Someone, you know,
Someone must keep alive that quality
Of living which separates us from the brutes;
And I have proposed it should be I.

DOMINIC. It should be me.

REEDBECK.   Beloved boy,
   It would be delightful if you thought so.

PERPETUA. I understand so far; I only wonder
   Why the Duke has to be . . . out of pocket.

REEDBECK. I care so much for civilization,
   Its patrician charm, its grave nobility;
   He cares so little. Therefore certain eccentric
   Means have had to be taken for splendid ends.
   Church and State, in a way, agree
   In justifying such a course of action.
   A kind of casual taxation. I hope I explain
   Quite clearly. It's true I have overlaid the Law
   With a certain transposition; we might
   Call this process Reedbequity. But what
   A gain to the world.

DOMINIC.   Do you hear that, Perpetua?
   He even unblushingly gives our name
   To his wicked practices!

PERPETUA.   Dominic wants us all
   To be good. Perhaps if you had gone to the Duke
   And explained all this, he would have eased the path
   To Reedbequity without the bother of iniquity.
   Don't you think he might?

REEDBECK. My dear, I've never believed
In the equal distribution of property.
I only think it can have more beauty
In my hands than in his. But that would have been
A most impertinent thing to say to him.

PERPETUA. We must keep you from harm. Heydee,
I'm not to be myself, I see.
I'm sad to see myself go;
But I was only promise, after all,
And the world can't live on that.

REEDBECK. Have you something that worries you? I believe
I've made you discontented with me, on a day
Which should have turned out so glorious, and now
I don't know *where* we are.

DOMINIC. It's only a step
From where you are, father, to where you will be
If we can't prevent it. You'll discover
Civilization is sadly dwindled when
You make your way to prison. Here's the Duke.
Be cheerful, if you can, Perpetua.

PERPETUA. My smile
Will be like the glint of handcuffs, but he's very
Welcome to it. Sing out a joke, Dominic,
In your merry way.

DOMINIC. Ssh!

PERPETUA. That's a most promising
Start to a conversation. There must be a joke
Lying about somewhere, even when the leaves are falling.

REEDBECK. Something about ... when the leaves in Eden fell ...

PERPETUA. Dear Poppadillo; thank you.

REEDBECK.   Was it at all
  Serviceable?

PERPETUA.   It had a kind of ancient virtue,
  Proper for this time and temple, yes.

       Enter the DUKE, *carrying a bow and quiver.*

DUKE. May your little girl come out and play, Reedbeck?
  Daylight is short, and becoming always shorter.
  But there's the space for an arrow or two between
  Now and the sunset.

PERPETUA.   I've never handled a bow.
  How shall I manage?

DUKE.   Beautifully.
  The light will hang fire to see you; you might
  Even hear the flash of the foliage
  Where Artemis parts the leaves to patronize
  And praise you; but take no notice, and watch what you're doing,
  And do what I tell you.

PERPETUA.   Implicitly.

DUKE.   Take notice
  Of the excellent marksmanship of the year, whose arrow
  Singing from the April bow crossed over the width
  Of summer straight for the gold, where now, if you look,
  You will see it quivering.

PERPETUA.   The year has a world of experience.
  But still, show me; and I'll try not to shame the shades
  Of all the arching duchesses and ladies
  Who played on these lawns before.

DUKE.   They'll arch the more,
  Adoring what you do, feathering their shafts
  And shooting until doomsday's Parthian shot.

                                        G

Be confident; and, if you miss,
The fashion of the game will be to miss,
Until you change your mind and hit.

> [*He begins to instruct her in the use of the bow, holding it with her, and speaking low into her ear, so that* REEDBECK *and* DOMINIC *cannot hear.*

And then, Perpetua, to-night
If a clear sky inclines you to it, and the heavens
Remain suspended, how would it be
If we trained the telescope on the infinite
And made what we could of what we could see of it?
Are you still as interested as you were
This morning?

PERPETUA.   Yes. I come from a city. The stars
Are new to me.

DUKE.   They shall answer you
By numbers. But we'll not tell the world
What we mean to do. There's a little tension to-day
Already, nerves perhaps not ready to accept
The quiet session of scientific study
You and I propose. So let's be as mute
As we're mutable, and avoid misapprehension.

PERPETUA. I—if so—if so—yes, very well.

DUKE. You can tell the world you need a long night of sleep.

PERPETUA. Yes, yes, I can. But here's the good afternoon light
Fading to waste unless we make use of it.

DUKE. I know that thought so well. Come on, then,
Let the trial begin.

PERPETUA.   Watch me, Poppadillo.
Come and judge what a huntress I should make,

What a rival for Artemis, and what chance Actaeon
Would have if I pursued him.

[*Exeunt the* DUKE *and* PERPETUA.

REEDBECK.   She really makes me
Respectful of astrology; it must
Have been the arrangement of stars she was born under.
It couldn't have been all me and her mother. Why,
I couldn't even dream so beautifully,
Let alone propagate. It must have been
The state of the zodiac when she was conceived.
But even so, I was there, and that in itself
Is remarkable. What did you say to her, Dominic;
What did you say to her?

DOMINIC.   I simply told her
You were crooked.

REEDBECK.   And then she said?

DOMINIC.   She said
She was not surprised.

REEDBECK.   Oh. *I* should have been;
It would have seemed like a thunder clap to *me*.
But you've made her feel differently towards me,
You've sent me off on my own again. And what
Did she mean by 'sad to see herself go', and 'not
To be herself any more'? What made her say that?
Was something agreed between you?

DOMINIC.   I made a point.

REEDBECK. What point, now what point?

DOMINIC.   I made the suggestion
She might like to marry the Duke, and save you that way.

REEDBECK. You—said—such a—thing? You dared

To consider selling your sister? You,
Sprung from my loins, and so utterly
Unprincipled?

DOMINIC.   That sounds most convincing,
Coming from you!

REEDBECK.   Poor little girl, poor
Little girl. But I'll intervene—*inter venio*,
Yes—though I can't relieve her
Of her inhuman brother.

DOMINIC.   Or her dishonest
Father.

REEDBECK [*shaking him, in a sudden burst of rage*]. You're a vain,
    vexing, incomprehensible,
Crimping, constipated duffer. What's your heart?
All plum duff! Why do I have to be
So inarticulate? God give me a few
Lithontriptical words! You grovelling little
Gobemouche!

DOMINIC.   Stop it, father, stop it at once!

REEDBECK. You spigoted, bigoted, operculated prig!

Enter JESSIE.

JESSIE. Am I in the way? I came to write a letter.

    [REEDBECK *releases* DOMINIC *suddenly, and* DOMINIC
    trips and falls sprawling on the floor.

REEDBECK. I was having a word with my son.

JESSIE [*to* DOMINIC].   How do you do?
Please don't bother to get up.

REEDBECK.   You're very welcome
To write your letter. I don't wish to shake him

Any more. But if you hadn't come in
I think I should have gone on shaking him
Until I couldn't see him.

JESSIE.   He would still
Have been there, of course. When my mother used to shake me
It always gave me hiccups, and then I was given
Peppermint on sugar to cure them. If only your son
Had hiccups, and you had peppermint and sugar,
Mr. Reedbeck, everything would seem different.

DOMINIC. I have to leave you. I'm afraid my father
Must be feeling very chastened and confused.

                                        [*Exit* DOMINIC.

JESSIE. It was lovely exercise for both of you.

REEDBECK. It did no good; I've only shaken my own
Composure.

JESSIE.   Sit down, Mr. Reedbeck, and let it settle.
I have to get a few lines off every day
To my father, eighty-seven. He can't read a word
Of my handwriting, and doesn't try, but he likes
The postman.

REEDBECK.   Well, I'll leave you, then;
I won't stop and hinder you. I suppose
That action of mine, that sudden accession of rage,
Wasn't in the nicest mood of civilization?
And yet I don't at all feel like apologizing,
I don't feel at all like apologizing. Would you apologize?

JESSIE. I'm sorry, I was trying to think how to begin
So that Dad won't mind he can't read it.

REEDBECK. Well, I won't stop and hinder you now,
But I should be very upset if I proved to be
Nothing but a barbarian after all,

A barbarian dreaming of the higher excellences.
But I won't stop and hinder you.

Enter HILDA.

Mrs. Dill
Is trying to write a letter. We mustn't hinder her.

[*Exit* REEDBECK.

HILDA. I see Hereward has made another backward
Flight into his heyday. It's a handsome thing
To see him so happy, but are we so happy for the girl?

JESSIE. Doesn't she like playing at bows and arrows?

HILDA. She does, no doubt, but—May I interrupt you?

JESSIE.   I'm only
Writing a letter when nothing else occurs to me;
I like to talk.

HILDA.   Because of the strange business
Of the eclipse this morning, and what went on,
We've been thrown into each other's confidence
Unexpectedly soon. And for my part
I think I'm thankful. I've always hidden more
Than was good for me, hoping in that way
To make my life seem pleasant to everyone,
But who should care? So I've lost the habit
Of daring to ask myself what I do, or why.
Why did I come here to-day, and what did I expect?
And why did he ever invite us here together?
I know him painstakingly enough
To be sure it was kindly meant; it couldn't have been
To watch our faces fall.

JESSIE.   I like being here
So much I never even wondered.

HILDA.   There
   Was still something in me to be hurt,
   Which a little surprised me. And then
   Reedbeck's daughter came, as though to show
   How the years had gone by for us
   But not for him, as though the old
   Magician in his blood was bound to draw us
   Into that revealing circle. But I sigh
   For her, as once I sighed for myself; and, if
   I knew how, I should tell her how lightly he flies.

JESSIE.   And then
   You must tell her how nicely he alights.
   That's important, too.
   I should let them be, because be they will.

HILDA. When I first met him, I remember, he seemed
   At once to give my spirits a holiday,
   Though (like a first holiday abroad) almost too unlike
   The daily round of the roundabout life I led—
   And lead still, O my heavens—which had, and has,
   All the appearance of movement without covering
   Any ground whatsoever. I know I have
   No particular heights or depths myself;
   No one who thought me ordinary or dull
   Would be far wrong. But even I despair
   For Roderic, my husband, who really is
   The height of depth, if it doesn't sound unkind
   To say so: not deep depth, but a level depth
   Of dullness. Once he had worn away the sheen
   Of his quite becoming boyhood, which made me fancy him,
   There was nothing to be seen in Roderic
   For mile after mile after mile, except
   A few sheeplike thoughts nibbling through the pages

Of a shiny weekly, any number of dead pheasants,
Partridges, pigeons, jays, and hares,
An occasional signpost of extreme prejudice
Marked 'No thoroughfare', and the flat horizon
Which is not so much an horizon
As a straight ruled line beyond which one doesn't look.

JESSIE. Keep him warm and fed. They bloom
Once in seven years.

HILDA.   Not Roderic.

Enter EDGAR, *carrying a bow and quiver.*

EDGAR. Are either of you ladies any good
At taking out a thorn? I took a look
In a mirror for some reason or other, and there it was.
A bramble slashed me when I was out riding yesterday.
I've brought my own needle.

HILDA.   Am I hurting you?

EDGAR. Yes, but how nice of you. Isn't it strange?
For the first time in my young life
I'm jealous of my father. I thought I'd better
Mention it before I begin to brood.

HILDA. Jealous of him, why?

EDGAR.   To me he's a man
Once and for all; once, once only,
And certainly for all. And any man
Who has to follow him (me, for instance)
Feels like the lag-last in a cloud of locusts:
By the time I come to a tree it's as bare
As a hat stand. Talent, conversation, wit,
Ease, and friendliness are all swallowed up
In advance. And just at present
I feel depressed about it.

HILDA.   Now, take heart.
  You have those virtues, too. There's room for both of you.

EDGAR. Not, I think, at the moment.

JESSIE.   Do you mean
  Only two can play at bows and arrows?

HILDA. I think at the moment it's greatly important
  There *should* be room for both of you. Suppose
  You make a bid for it. Why not?
  Nothing hinders you except weakness of hope,
  And that's ridiculous. We'll go together.
  Mrs. Dill wants to write a letter.

JESSIE.   Never mind;
  Everything writes itself in time.

Enter BATES.

BATES. It's Mrs. Taylor-Snell I'm looking for;
  Oh, that's right, lady, you're here. I have
  A message to give you, they said; prompto.
  On the telephone it come. It's not so nice
  As you might like to have it, but it's not so bad.
  It seems there's been a bit of a accident,
  And they'd be glad if you could make it convenient
  To find your way back 'ome.

HILDA.   Roderic!

BATES. Whoever it is, missis, you're not to worry.
  Your old man has got hisself throwed off his horse,
  Hunting little rabbits and uvver breeders.
  Now, now, lady, you never know,
  It may only be a front toof a bit loose.

HILDA. Didn't they say what the injury was?

BATES. Took a bit of a toss, come a bit of a purler,
  What Jack and Jill done; don't you worry, lady.

HILDA. I can't help worrying, dear Bates. [*To* JESSIE] I'll go
  Without saying good-bye to Hereward. There's no reason
  Why anyone's afternoon should suffer,
  Except mine; and later I'll telephone
  And tell you what has happened.

JESSIE.   It's wretched for you,
  It's really wretched for you; I'm awfully sorry.
  What would you like me to do?

HILDA.   Nothing, except
  To forget I laughed at him. I have my car;
  I can slip away easily.

EDGAR.   I'll run on ahead
  And get the car started for you.

HILDA.   No.
  Thank you, but I'd rather go quietly alone.
  If you want to do something for me, put your shoulders
  To your father, and make yourself your own success.
  Good-bye.

EDGAR.   Good-bye, good luck.

JESSIE.   I expect you'll find
  It's something nice and simple like a collar-bone.
                                    [*Exit* HILDA.
  Oh, please God, make it a collar-bone. She turned
  So pale and unhappy, poor lamb.

BATES. I wouldn't have anything happen to that one:
  It's a pity we can't do something to oblige her.
  But there's that uvver one, Fleming she says she's called:
  Flaming nuisance, I reply: what about her,
  Eh, miss? What's she doing snooping

About the east wing all the afternoon? I tell you,
Miss, I knows an undesirable character
When I see one; I've been one myself for years.

JESSIE. And look how we love you. So don't you have
Nasty thoughts about Miss Fleming, who is not
Undesirable at all. And go away
Like a good boy, and let me write my letter.

BATES. I just fought you might like the opinion of a expert.

[*He begins wandering away.*

But don't let's say anyfing good about
Captain Fussing Reddleman, lord of the kitchens.
He can go and tame his lions on some uvver poor bastard's mug.
I prefers to keep mine natural.

[*Exit* BATES.

EDGAR. I wonder if I should.

JESSIE.   If you should what?

EDGAR. From here I think I could send an arrow right past him
Into the target.

JESSIE.   If you think you can, then do.

[EDGAR *takes an arrow, fits it in his bow, and shoots. A
distant cry of remonstrance from the* DUKE.

EDGAR. Oh, that was very beautiful. I enjoyed that
Extremely.

JESSIE.   What did you do? Did I encourage you
To be mischievous? I was thinking about my letter.
You might have shot your father.

EDGAR.   I jolly nearly
Did. But my arrows, I never quite know why,
Have a considerate way of going where
I mean them to go, which was nearer the gold than his.
He's probably shooting not so well

To give Perpetua some encouragement.
When I come to think of it, that shot of mine
Was taking a very easy advantage.

JESSIE. I shouldn't say easy, twice the distance off.
And as you didn't kill anybody, I may say
I think it was splendid, and I think perhaps
You should do it more often.

Enter the DUKE.

DUKE. What, by Saint Sebastian's groin,
Do you think you're up to? Edgar, for goodness' sake!

EDGAR. I was drawing a bow at a venture, father.

DUKE.   So
I thought. But remember what damage was done to Sir Lancelot
By an arrow in the buttocks. Did I beget you
To be shot from behind?

EDGAR.   I'm extremely sorry,
But you took a step to the south.

DUKE.   Am I never to move?

EDGAR. Oh, yes, father, but the other way, or any way
Except between me and where I aim.

DUKE.   I hope
I'm being patient. I had quite supposed
The contest was between Miss Reedbeck and me.

EDGAR. When all the time it was really between you
And your loving son; or so my hackles tell me.

DUKE. Ah—! Now I see;
Your days are starting to press upon me,
You who were always so unassuming and easy.
But not this time. No, I'm sorry,
Not this time, Edgar.

EDGAR. It is this time.
I'm sorry, too, but it is this time. You've had
A long innings, and a summer of splendid outings,
And now I must ask you, father, not to monopolize
Every heart in the world any longer.

JESSIE. Excuse me
Worrying you, but how do you spell epidemic?
Two *p*'s and two *m*'s?

EDGAR. I'd forgotten we weren't alone.

DUKE. We're alone with Jessie; nothing could be happier.
One *p*, one *m*. If the generations join
In a life-and-death struggle under your feet
Don't let it, Jessie, disturb your spelling.

JESSIE. One *p*, one *m*. Quite enough, when you look at it.

DUKE. Now listen, Edgar, take nothing for granted,
Not even my flair for breaking into love;
You're apprehensive far too soon. The field,
If not entirely yours, is not entirely mine:
I am as innocently there
As an old warhorse put out to grass:
My equine equability is pastoral to a fault.

EDGAR. But when you're grazing you're irresistible;
Buttercups and daisies fall to your fetlocks in swathes;
I've seen it happen. And between this morning's eclipse
And this afternoon you've lost the autumnal look
Which was such a comfort to me; I see you have
The appearance of a very mild March day.
And what does a boy do then?

DUKE. Aren't you being
Just a thought parricidal for a fine afternoon?

EDGAR. Oh, God, I love you like the rest of them.
I'm only asking you to forgo yourself
This once, to suspend your animation
For a few short months, for my sake.

DUKE.   Edgar,
I mean to be a good father to you, but
A good father must be a man. And what
Is a man? Edgar, what is a man? O
My man-child, what in the world is a man?
Speaking for myself, I am precisely that question:
I exist to know that I exist
Interrogatively. But what gives birth
To a question? A desire to be answered. A question
Desires, as a man must desire, as I
Desire. That, at least, you'll allow me.
You wouldn't have your father merely rhetorical.

EDGAR. Not at all, but——

DUKE.   But what is the mark of the question?
What is the note of this interrogation?
Loneliness. The note, my son, is loneliness.
Over all the world
Men move unhoming, and eternally
Concerned: a swarm of bees who have lost their queen.
Nothing else is so ill at ease. We know
How patiently the toad suns on the stone,
How the indolent fish waves its tail in time
With the waving weed. If a pulse was in the stone,
And the stone grew moist, and the toad petrified,
Patience would still be as patient in the sun.
Or if the weed wove its way up river
To breed, and the fish waved green and still,
The water would never wonder: all

Is at one with the rest.
And the trees, when the weather is waking, quicken without
Question, their leaves assemble in a perfect faith
Of summer; and so with all the world's life,
Except ours. We can hear the lyric lark
Flaking its limit of heaven from a cloud,
And see the self-assimilated cat,
The adaptable chameleon, and the mole
Rubbing along companionably
With the obliging earth. But where, O Edgar,
Is an element compatible with *us*?

EDGAR. Would you mind if I reminded you, father,
What we were talking about when you started talking?

DUKE. Thank you, but I know: your wish to remove me.
But if being alive is a question, heaven-bent
For an answer, and the question is a man's
Estrangement in a world
Where everything else conforms, how should I dare
To suspend myself for a day, or even an hour,
When that hour might ravish me
Into a complete, unsolitary life,
Where happiness leaves no room for the restless mind
And I, as unlaborious
As a laburnum tree, hang in caresses of gold.

EDGAR. And what do I hang in?

DUKE.   You hang in abeyance, Edgar.
If I should die, with the great question unanswered,
I leave myself in you to ask it still.
But this is all academic. The field is still open.

JESSIE. I always think 'niece' is such a difficult word.

DUKE. *I* before *E*, except after *C*. And so,
Edgar, let nothing dismay you——

JESSIE.   Except
In the case of 'neigh', that humorous noise of a horse.

Enter PERPETUA.

PERPETUA. Is archery all over? I went to the lake
And tried to spear fish with an arrow, but I'm tired
Of that.

DUKE.   Edgar, I'm nowhere to be seen;
For all the personality I exert
You might never have had a father; advance, advance,
You son of a cipher.

PERPETUA.   Could we not all shoot together?

EDGAR. Miss Reedbeck——

PERPETUA.   Perpetua.

EDGAR.   Yes. Perpetua,
This is All Hallowe'en. To-night half England
Will be dancing in memory of a world they don't remember.
The sky will very likely be black with broomsticks.
There's a dance on in the Old Woolmarket
At Mordenbury. Will you come?

PERPETUA [*glancing towards the* DUKE]. All Hallowe'en.
I should have liked it dearly, but to-night——

EDGAR. You've made some other plan.

PERPETUA.   No, no.

EDGAR. Then come. Meet England first among the wisps
Of magic we still possess. Will you, Perpetua?

PERPETUA. If I dared to trust my eyes and my feet
To be lively, so long after sunset,
I should say yes willingly. But I must and will
Sleep early. Four days on the see-saw sea,

And then such a wave of homecoming, have left me
Ready to rest. I'm so sorry to refuse.

EDGAR. Well, I see you must, though I'm very sad you must.
But if later you should feel revived, or if
You found you could rest before dinner——

PERPETUA. It still has to be no, and still I'm sorry.

EDGAR. I can well imagine how tired you are. You can let
Your sleep make you a Hallowe'en instead.
Dreams know where to look for deeper and stranger
Shadows than I do. Horses, it always seems
To me, are half a dream, even when
You have them under your hand, and when I *dream* them
They tremble and sweat, the caves of their nostrils blowing
Bright clouds of breath, a foaming sea
Breaks against their mouths, their flanks are smoking
Like Abel's fire to heaven, as though
A dreadful necessity had ridden them hard
Through the miles of my sleep, all the benighted way
From legend into life. And then in the morning
There they are in the stables, waiting to be blessed.

PERPETUA. Show me these wonders.

EDGAR.   Now?

PERPETUA.   Yes, why not now?
All of us.

EDGAR.   That goes for you, papa.

DUKE. Invisibly I come.

EDGAR [*glumly*].   Invisibility
Makes you look younger than ever.

                      [*Exit* PERPETUA *and* EDGAR.

DUKE.   Jessie,
Will you make an end of dotting your *i*'s and join us?

JESSIE. Thank you, dear,
   But I'd like to finish this letter to my father,
   Even though he'll never read it.

DUKE.   Jessie, my love,
   If he'll never read it, do you have to write so much?

JESSIE. Well, no, but he lives such a long way out of the village
   I like to make it worth the postman's while.

                        Enter ROSABEL.

DUKE. Rosabel, where have you been mooning
   All the long afternoon? Come with your friends
   And look at horses. Edgar is showing Miss Reedbeck
   Round the stables.

ROSABEL.   Yes, yes, I may follow you—
   When do you mean to show her how to observe
   The stars through your telescope? Is it to-night?

DUKE. No, not to-night; sometime, perhaps, or perhaps
   Never; who can say?

ROSABEL.   But *you* will be there, I suppose.
   Who is it that's mooning then? And all night long?
   And making the world look small and apologetic
   And as good as unpopulated? I hate your telescope!

DUKE. So you have said. Don't let it obsess you.
   Look up, Mrs. Siddons, it's easy enough
   To see over the top of a telescope. So try,
   Or you'll soon make yourself ill. Anyway
   I'm washing my hands of all the sky to-night,
   And I'm going early to bed.
                                         [*Exit the* DUKE.

ROSABEL [*to herself*].   So no one at all
   Will be there. Now I know why all day long

Life has been tilting and driving me towards
To-night. I'm not myself any more,
I am only the meaning of what comes after dark,
If I have the courage.

> [*She remembers* JESSIE *and turns to her.*

Obsessed, obsessed.
It's very true. One thought in my head,
Persevering like someone running on a race-track;
When it seems to be going it's coming again.
I wrestle with it, and hold it close,
I can't let it go, nor laugh it away. Is this
How men get driven to send history lurching on
To God knows where? Nothing matters
Except that he should be made to feel. He hurts
Whoever he touches. He has to be touched by fire
To make a human of him, and only a woman
Who loves him can dare to do it.

JESSIE.   Listen, love,
You'll be sending yourself silly. I always think
When someone knocks you down, it doesn't improve things
To knock yourself up. The way a thing is, is often
The way you happen to look at it. He's as kind
As anybody living, if you take a running jump.
And if you only had a stamp we could go together
And put this in the box.

ROSABEL.   I'm over-run
By the most curious thoughts. I believe I was kept
From quite succeeding in anything I set
My heart on, so that now I should give all
My heart to this, to-night. The girl Perpetua
Has the courage that makes a person come true.
Did you hear her say how she went to war on things

She hated? I think she came to show me
What it is I have to do; indeed, I can't do less!
And nothing less will do to open his eyes
On to the distances that separate him
From other people.

JESSIE.　　　　　　　　Look at me: I've put Cumberland
When I mean Northants.

ROSABEL.　　　　　　　To-night, no one is there.
You'll see, I shall send his Observatory
Where Nero's Rome has gone; I'll blaze a trail
That he can follow towards humanity!

JESSIE. Now I wonder who's the most likely person to have a
stamp?

THE CURTAIN FALLS

SCENE TWO

The Observatory Room at night. The DUKE *is lying on a day-bed in the
dark. Enter* PERPETUA. *The light from the corridor follows her
a little way into the room. She stands uncertain. The* DUKE
speaks from the darkness.

DUKE. And Endymion, when the moon had borne him
Fifty daughters, was rewarded with
An eternal siesta; his breast and belly rose
And fell like the sea; his breath played
All day with the motes of the dust,
While all about him suffered, withered, and crumbled
Into the dust his breath played with; only,
Between the slats of his perfect sleep
Came little slants of sun, and they were muddy
With the hard wading of humanity;

This made him change his position slightly,
And that stirred up the scent of the thyme which made
His unimpassioned bed.

PERPETUA.   It's rather frightening
When a dark room starts to speak.

DUKE.   My original
Syntax, like original sin, grows vastier
In the dark. Come in.

PERPETUA.   What does your legend mean?

DUKE. It means, Perpetua, we're all as well
As can be expected. Does anyone know you're here?

PERPETUA. No one.

DUKE.   They would think I meant to love you.
I wonder if I mean any such thing.
We'll make some light. Matches?

PERPETUA.   No.

DUKE. No, here are some.
                    [*He lights an oil lamp.*
                This was the first
Astonishment of creation; after that
Came the frenzy of which you and I
Are the humble result. An access of starlight
And the fish began to swim; God gave way
To hallucinations; you and I again.
Would you like a drink?

PERPETUA.   Thank you. Tell me, as one
Hallucination to another, what
Happiness do you get up here with your telescope?

DUKE. I can't remember. That's a handsome moth
Come in to die, two petals, two tendrils,

And a flake of snow, meticulous, irrelevant,
Unwise. You came to see my stars. I have them
Here.

PERPETUA. I expect you can find your way about them
Even in the dark. Tell me who it is
We're trained on now.

DUKE.   Senator Saturn, white-
Hot with gravity. His moon, out of love
For his grey steel brow,
Streamed away her life into a circle
Of tormented arms. You see them there,
You see how they circle and never touch.
Saturn is alone, for all their circling round him.

PERPETUA. And alone so long. I'm looking at the same star
That shone alone in the wake of Noah's
Drifting ark as soon as the rain was over,
That shone on shining Charlemagne
Far away, and as clear
As the note of Roland's homing horn.
Alone so long, and now casually
Descending to us, on a Thursday midnight:
Saturn, who once glinted in the glass
Of Ariadne's mirror at the moment
When she died and melted out of Naxos.

DUKE. Ariadne died in childbirth. One
Life put the other out. It was Edgar's mode
Of entrance. Where in the sky shall we go to now?

PERPETUA. Wherever you may like to take me. I'm
A stranger here.

DUKE.   She died a girl in love,
And I went on in love without her

For longer than was fair. But this is not
Astronomy.

PERPETUA.   Astrology, then. You can't
Throw someone against the sky and not expect
A certain vapour of magic to condense
In moisture on their lashes. Let me believe
For a little while in man's ordeal by star
And tell me your own. I want to hear it.

DUKE. Isn't it a strange love, Perpetua,
That will never, can never, know what it was?
Death chose to interrupt us while we were still
Careening together high above the spires
Of common sense. And so what modulation
Would have come, how soon, how scaling down,
Is never to be known. And I can never tell
Whether a love, which was haled away
While it still was hale, was all and more
Of love than I could expect again: or if
The one twin-hearted permanence
Was waiting somewhere ahead. That has always
Perplexed me. What have I been doing, since
She died? Making do because the best
Was done? Or have I been turning head by head
To find the face which, willingly,
I should never let pass? For a long while now
I've been thinking the first, but to-day
The question seems to have sprung into life again.

PERPETUA. With your mind so full of inquiry, I'm surprised
You've had any time for love.

DUKE.   It takes no time.
It's on us while we walk, or in mid-sentence,

A sudden hoarseness, enough to choke the sense.
Now isn't that so?

PERPETUA.   Not so with me.

DUKE.   You must try
To use longer sentences. Then you would certainly feel
The fumbling in the quiver behind every syllable
And so to the arrow sting, like a sudden
Swerving parenthesis.

PERPETUA.   Do you think I should?

DUKE. No doubt of it.

PERPETUA.   There isn't any reason
Why a sentence, I suppose, once it begins,
Once it has risen to the lips at all
And finds itself happily wandering
Through shady vowels and over consonants
Where ink's been spilt like rivers or like blood
Flowing for the cause of some half-truth
Or a dogma now outmoded, shouldn't go
Endlessly moving in grave periphrasis
And phrase in linking phrase, with commas falling
As airily as lime flowers, intermittently,
Uninterrupting, scarcely troubling
The mild and fragile progress of the sense
Which trills trebling like a pebbled stream
Or lowers towards an oath-intoning ocean
Or with a careless and forgetful music
Looping and threading, tuning and entwining,
Flings a babel of bells, a carolling
Of such various vowels the ear can almost feel
The soul of sound when it lay in chaos yearning
For the tongue to be created: such a hymn
If not as lovely, then as interminable,

As restless, and as heartless, as the hymn
Which in the tower of heaven the muted spheres
With every rippling harp and windy horn
Played for incidental harmony
Over the mouldering rafters of the world,
Rafters which seldom care to ring, preferring
The functional death-watch beetle, stark, staccato,
Economical as a knuckle bone,
Strict, correct, but undelighting
Like a cleric jigging in the saturnalia,
The saturnalia we all must keep,
Green-growing and rash with life,
Our milchy, mortal, auroral, jovial,
Harsh, unedifying world,
Where every circle of grass can show a dragon
And every pool's as populous as Penge,
Where birds, with taffeta flying, scarf the air
On autumn evenings, and a sentence once
Begun goes on and on, there being no reason
To draw to any conclusion so long as breath
Shall last, except that breath
Can't last much longer.

DUKE.   Now point me out the comma
Where you loved me.

PERPETUA.   Not at any.

DUKE.   Let me see;
Was there a colon somewhere?

PERPETUA.   Perhaps one;
But if so we passed it without any trouble
Of any sort.

DUKE.   Never mind. There are sure

To be other sentences. The little god
Is older than he was, and moves more slowly.

PERPETUA. Even when he aims at you?

DUKE.   For me, I'm afraid,
He makes a special effort, shoots
Most generously, and then, poor boy, can't handle
A bow for several weeks.

PERPETUA.   Why are you so sure
That I must love you? The field is wide,
And everyone's heart is a great eccentric;
Its whole distinction is a madness. Wildly
Away from any mark it goes, making
Anywhere the same gigantic mimicry of sunshine,
No one else knows why. Be sure of nothing.

DUKE. Do you know what night this is?

PERPETUA.   All-Hallows Eve.

DUKE. All-Hallows Eve. If the earth is ever wise
To magic, this is the night when magic's wisdom
Comes rolling in across our sedate equation.
All the closed hours unlock; the rigorous ground
Grows as soft as the sea, exhaling
The bloom of the dead everywhere. They almost
Live again: as nearly, at least, as we
Can brush on death. And through the night
They trespass agreeably on our time of trespasses,
Molesting the air in a pale, disinterested
Way, until they thankfully notice
The dark is paler, and sigh themselves out again;
Though not before they've planted, as they go,
A seed of chill which grows rapidly
Into a rigid winter where the sun

Can hardly raise himself to make a noon.
But still, that's presently. What's more to our purpose
Is that to-night the gravity of mirrors
Is so potent it can draw the future
Into the glass, and show shadows of husbands
To girls who sit and comb their hair. Suppose
You try it.

PERPETUA.   I'm two or three centuries
Too late.

DUKE.   We know nothing yet.
There's the mirror. In your bag no doubt
A comb. And while you comb tradition says
You must eat an apple: though God knows why
Any apple should trust itself between your teeth
After this morning's little episode.
However, here's one intrepid to the core.

PERPETUA. How old is this mirror? The glass
Is very loath to let me in.

DUKE.   Eight duchesses
Have rested there in passing, before the glass
Began to cloud; and after that came three
Peering housekeepers, a chambermaid
Who, what with frequent tears and the ageing mirror,
Never saw her face; and me, who by
Much early study have overcome the need
To try.

PERPETUA. And I am the eight duchesses
And the three housekeepers and the chambermaid
Combing their hair. I am any girl: Perpetua
Perpetual, making no gesture I can call
My own, engraving theirs one lifetime deeper.

Midnight, the apple, and Perpetua
Combing her hair, as all the time she was.

> [*The* DUKE *quietly crosses the room until his reflection falls
> into the mirror.* PERPETUA'S *attention is caught; she stares
> into the glass before she turns suddenly to look at the* DUKE.

It seemed to be your son.

DUKE.   Perpetua,
You must play fair.

PERPETUA.   You must tell that to the mirror.
The reflection seemed to be Edgar.

DUKE.   Then the mirror
Is very penetrating. It has seen
How young, to all intents, I am.

PERPETUA.   I suppose so.
You think there's no magic.

DUKE.   That's as kind
As anything you've said. I think there *is*
Magic: an old dim-sighted mirror
And a shaded lamp for one genial moment
Raised me out of the falling leaves. A pity
The vision has gone. I'll agree to immortality
If immortality is to be always twenty-five
Seen by a man approaching fifty. The thought
Alone sends me begging to Olympus.
And you, being twenty-five, and looked upon
By me, together we make one golden flesh
For which both worlds, this and the next, will try
To outbid each other, and while the bidding mounts
We'll spend our love between them, disregarding
Both, until——

PERPETUA.   Until, next year,
I am twenty-six.

DUKE.   Which is twenty-five and one more.
I am the one.

PERPETUA.   It remains for me to love you.

DUKE. It has always been understood to be so easy.
Why ever should you not? Am I, before
God, too old? Consider the rocks
Of Arizona, and then consider me.
How recently the world has had the pleasure
Of pleasing, the opportunity of knowing me.
Age, after all, is only the accumulation
Of extensive childhood: what we were,
Never what we are. Don't deliver me
Up to my grey hairs.

PERPETUA.   Them I could certainly
Love. No, it's rather that I wonder
Whether you're not almost too young to be lived with.

DUKE. When we're married I shall age beside you; forgive me
Loitering now till you draw level.

PERPETUA. When we're married?

DUKE.   Are we to be formal?
Should I have asked you first?

PERPETUA.   Not if you have
Some other way of knowing the answer. Have you?

DUKE. Perhaps I may pass that question back. Have I?

PERPETUA. Your Grace——

DUKE.   Somewhere I have a Christian name.

PERPETUA. Do you know anything against my father?

DUKE. In my heart, nothing.
He loves me in his way, and that absolves him
From any defect on earth. No doubt
He'll have to stand in a corner of heaven with his face
To a jasper wall, but here let him thrive.

PERPETUA.   You mean
You know.

DUKE.   I know he wishes to make honey.
Any bee would tell you, that's impossible
If clover objects to rape.

PERPETUA.   So this is how
You know I shall marry you: for Poppadillo's sake?

DUKE. This is how.

PERPETUA.   And perhaps it is going to feel
Strange to you at first to know I am not.
No, no, you're mistaken, and I was quite
Mistaken, too! This isn't how I mean
To lose my way, by force of circumstantial
Evidence. When I lose my way I shall lose it
In my own time, and by my own misguided
Sense of direction.

DUKE.   Planting your own brambles,
Digging your own pitfalls, willing your own
Will-o'-the-wisps, designing
Down to the last detail Perpetua's Folly.

PERPETUA. Without respect of persons. But do you mean
You have sat perched up here, for months and years,
Your eyes shrewdly glittering with starlight,
Knowing that my father, fifty feet below,
Was being clever in your clover, and you said
Nothing?

DUKE.   We were being so happy together.
And if I had mentioned it, he would have felt
Obliged to discontinue, which would have been
Immensely sad. And, what is more,
Swarming stars and solitary Duke
Would have been unvisited to-night.

PERPETUA. How happy do you feel to know you tried
For a bride by this conspiracy of silence?

DUKE. How happy do you feel to know you were ready
To take a husband to make that silence absolute?

PERPETUA. I made no pretence of loving you. I was glad
When Edgar came to the mirror; I don't know why.

DUKE. I seem to have come to the end of myself
Sooner than I expected. So there's to be
No climax and adorable close
With ego agonistes crowned and smiling?
The strange charm of being alive breaks off
Abruptly, with nothing determined, nothing solved,
No absolute anything. I thought this time
The ends of the ring would join. But, no,
I'm back among the fragments.

PERPETUA.   Is this fair?

DUKE. How nature loves the incomplete. She knows
If she drew a conclusion it would finish her.
But, O God, for one round Amen!

PERPETUA.   That only
Comes on judgement day, and so,
As love won't live with judgement, Amen must wait.
Show me one more star and I must go.

DUKE. I think they're falling.

While I love you without being loved they're sure
To be restive.

PERPETUA. When they fall do they scorch the air
In passing? Is that what I can smell?

DUKE.   Or is it
The smell of man being born to trouble? Or both
The upward sparks and the downward stars together?

PERPETUA. Something *is* on fire. I can hear the flames
Crunching on wood.

DUKE.   Have my almost mindless gardeners
Been suddenly visited by imagination
And lit us a Hallowe'en bonfire?

PERPETUA.   Why, look, the garden's
Capering with light. The fire is underneath us—
Look! It's the house, this wing of the house is on fire!

DUKE. Merciful heaven,
Wouldn't you think my blood was warm enough
To get us through a night without encouragement?

PERPETUA. Shall we be able to get away?

DUKE.   By all means.
We'll leave the moths to perform whatever
Immolation is necessary. A more
Temperate life is better for us,
And the cooler coast of the garden.

   [*He throws open the door and looks on to the stairs.*

Well, here's a riproaring gauntlet to be run
By a couple of God's children.

PERPETUA.   No! No, no!
Not that way!

DUKE. Which other? The only alternative
To downward is upward, and how do you propose
Two such wingless babes as we are—
No, Perpetua; quickly, love, before
The even chance is out of patience with us.

PERPETUA. No! There's no chance there. You can see
There's no chance there. It's all in the fire,
Every tread of the stairs. What shall we do?

[*She runs to the window and looks down.*

So far away, so far away.

DUKE. Trust me;
Try this way in my arms, Perpetua. Hope
Is forlorn, but I'm sure very fond of us.
We'll give her the benefit, shall we, and both be brave?

PERPETUA. Don't make me. I'd rather jump to the garden, and die
Fair and broken. I'll make my own death
As it suits me.

DUKE. That as well? I'm sorry; you can have
Your own way in everything else.

PERPETUA. Please,
Please, please, please.

DUKE. Well, I see
We've chosen. Hope has got tired of waiting
And taken half the staircase with her. Now,
We'll ring a rescue, and then indulge in the luxury
Of having nothing to do but fold our hands.

[*He holds her beside him while he uses the telephone.*

Gently, my dear, you White Queen; nothing
Has hurt us yet. A fire at Stellmere Park.
Two people trapped: neither anxious to die.

H

I suggest you should make remarkable speed.
God bless you. They didn't wait for blessing.

PERPETUA. Aren't you desperate, too? Aren't you even afraid?

DUKE. Why, yes, yes, I have to be; I love myself,
And I shall be sad to say good-bye to myself;
There's no one like me, though so many better.
Will you kiss the last of a singular man?

PERPETUA. Easily, oh, easily.

DUKE.   There's always a good thing left
Even when the world would seem to be spent out.
Do you think you love me?

PERPETUA.   Yes, I love you:
Between the giddiness I love you.

DUKE.   May it also
Be between my arms? I love my love
With a death because it has no alteration
And no end. This concluding grace, Amen.
In the long world we're being shaken from
The star which, when it's rising, is called Venus,
Setting is Lucifer, the goddess
Graduating into demon, and what good
Is that for a man's immortal spirit? But you
And I, pursuing love no farther than this
Pure outcry of recognition,
Possess it most faithfully.

PERPETUA.   I only know—
Listen to the fire now, listen to it!
It means to let nothing escape. I only know
We go together into pain.

DUKE. Out of the world like snow. And so
The phoenix and the turtle did.

Pain took them, too, and welded them
And melted them, and made a union
Of beauty born and beauty reft away,
And, when the air was empty, time was brimming,
And light was beating with one heart.

PERPETUA. I'm afraid of the fire, I'm afraid, I am so
Afraid of the fire.

[*The voice of* REDDLEMAN *is heard outside the door.*

REDDLEMAN [*off*]. Your Grace! All right, all right, your Grace!

DUKE. The voice of to-morrow morning, after all.
We're not to be allowed perfection, Perpetua.
The kind world intervenes.

Enter REDDLEMAN.

REDDLEMAN. Ah, you poor sinners. I'm with you now;
Did you think I was never coming?

PERPETUA.   Never coming,
Never, never coming!

DUKE.   Quietly yet,
Fly up gently, we've still got far to go.
How do you propose to rescue us, Reddleman?
And how the hell did you get here?

REDDLEMAN: By me flair
For elementary science. I thumbed a lift
On the rising heat. And, by the blistering
Of the blessed St. Laurence and the blessed St. Vincent,
Shadrac, Meshac, Abednego, and all
The sainted salamanders, I've got me nerve again;
For there's the conflagration below, frumping
And grouching like all the golden lads of lions
I ever put me hand into the fire of!

Didn't God make sinners of you and trap you here
For the decent purpose of putting me back
In the way of salvation?

DUKE.   And us, too, I hope.
Can we go the way you came?

PERPETUA.   God be kind,
Be kind.

REDDLEMAN. Have you any objection, now,
To dropping from time to time into me arms
From a great way off? 'Twould be to avoid the stairs,
Themselves being gone entirely.

PERPETUA. Must it be that way?

REDDLEMAN.   In the Captain's keeping,
Via Leo, con brio, the way of the lions!

DUKE. He's got himself well up in the god class now,
Perpetua: all we have to do is trust ourselves
To the rope of his nerve, spit on our hands, and go.

                          [BATES *appears at the window.*

BATES. Well, *you've* got yourselves in a picklin' walls-up
And no mistake.

DUKE.   Are we to have all
The guardian angels at a blow?
You spoil us, Bates.

REDDLEMAN.   He spoils me night of glory.
Send him about his business, if you love me,
Your Grace, for the love of God, send him
About his business!

BATES.   Couldn't the Lord Lieutenant
Even keep his nose out of this little job?

Come on, miss; come and take a butcher's
At the panorama; it's lovely outside 'ere.

PERPETUA. Oh, yes, yes!

REDDLEMAN. Monkeys, monkeys, monkeys!

DUKE. How do you think we're going to get down, Bates?

BATES. Well, I come up by the ladders, but according
To the rules we have to slip down by the snakes. Still,
Do what your fancy tells you, mate. I'm
Not looking.

PERPETUA. And I wish I hadn't looked, and I wish
We were safe on the ground.

DUKE. Think of something high
Like Kanchenjunga. That very nearly takes us
Down the ladder before we start.

REDDLEMAN. Your Grace,
You're not so out of your mind as to go
Out of the window? Encouraging robbery
And violence, you are, to set your foot
On a ladder propped up against your property
Without permission, and in the middle of the night
When no decent man would be lashing one ladder
To another, and he in his shirt.

BATES. You save 'em
Wiv your trousers, go on, let's see you; save 'em wiv your
trousers.

DUKE. Reddleman, by all means love your lions,
But condescend to the snakes. Come on.

REDDLEMAN. Where's a fine soul under heaven?

DUKE. Not playing
With fire, wherever else he may be.

BATES.   That's right, miss,
Let me take you, miss; fink nuffing of it.
Relax yourself, as though you was mink.
Fink lovely foughts, miss, and you won't weigh nuffing.
Wonder what stretch I'll have to do for abduction?

DUKE [*climbing through the window after them*]. A beautiful room,
    Reddleman; worth a fortune
In memories and astronomical equipment.

                [*He disappears from view.* REDDLEMAN *leans out.*

REDDLEMAN. H'wot do you think the dear God gave me back
Me nerve for? To come crawling after heathen
Like spittle down a window? B'Jason,
I've a better opinion of meself.
Anyway, it makes me giddy and it's no position
For any reasonable man to get himself into.

    [*He crosses the room, throws open the door, and meets the
    glare of the fire.*

Tossing your mighty manes, roaring yellow murder!
The Captain's not afraid!

    [*Exit* REDDLEMAN. *The* DUKE *climbs back in at the win-
    dow calling him, races across the room to the door, calls:*

DUKE. Reddleman, you hell-raking maniac!

    [*He picks up the half-eaten apple from the dressing table, calls
    to* REDDLEMAN:

Who would have the heart to disappoint you?

    [*He puts the apple between his teeth and follows* REDDLE-
    MAN *the way of the stairs.*

THE CURTAIN FALLS ON ACT TWO

ACT THREE

The Temple of the Ancient Virtues, an hour or so later. The light from the burning house reflected in the lake. ROSABEL *is sobbing in the dark. Enter* DOMINIC, *carrying two chairs and a stable lantern. He halts and listens to the sobbing.*

DOMINIC. May I interrupt your unhappiness,
Just to bring in one or two things? It's begun
To rain. Everything's going to get wet.
I wonder if you need cry quite so despairingly.
It makes me feel very awkward. I am not good
At comforting people, even when I know
Where to look for them. I'm Dominic Reedbeck . . .
How do you do? And where would you be?

ROSABEL. Oh, no,
Don't look for me.

DOMINIC. I couldn't look for you;
I don't know who you are. Everyone
Is safe, you know; they're all accounted for,
Except Miss Fleming. Do you know where she is?

ROSABEL. No. No one must ever see her again.

DOMINIC. Why not? Is she so badly burned? What is it,
Oh, what *is* it? I wish you'd help me to be helpful;
I find it so difficult.

ROSABEL. I'm here. I wish
I were dead.

DOMINIC. I don't see how you can wish for something
You only know the name of. Now that it's raining

I won't be the only one coming in here. Perhaps
You should try to feel better. If I were you.

ROSABEL. They wouldn't look for me in hell.

DOMINIC.   Oh, yes, they would.
It's the obvious place to look for anyone,
If you're speaking euphemistically.

ROSABEL. I'm grateful to you. So would anyone
In hell be. Your voice is very cold.
I want harshness. I want hatred.
If you would hate me it might help me to bear
To think of myself. You're going to find it easy.
It was I who started the fire. I did it
Deliberately.

DOMINIC.   Perpetua was there.
The Duke was there. They might never have got away.

ROSABEL. But you haven't understood. You can't have understood
It was I who did this unimaginable thing.

DOMINIC. I was thinking of myself.
My sister was there because I sent her there.
Perhaps you were compelled to be the means
By which I was shown I had fallen into error.
If so, I must thank you. Thank you, Miss Fleming.

ROSABEL. You're mad! Do you think I hurled myself away
From all the decent world for your sake?
Hate me, hate me! Oh, why is it
You won't understand?

DOMINIC.   I do understand. I know
Too well our preternatural aptitude
For sin. My father made it quite clear to me.

ROSABEL. Oh, what shall I do?

DOMINIC.   There's Sergeant Harry Bullen,
The policeman from Swinford Magna. He's a very
Reasonable chap; I'm sure he'd arrest you
Willingly if you went and asked him.
And he's here, which is very convenient for you.

ROSABEL. Yes, where? Where is he?

DOMINIC.   I saw him five minutes ago,
Coming head first down a ladder, to show the Duke
(As he said) that in the ordinary course of living
It makes little difference which way up you are.
He was joking, I think.

ROSABEL.   I'll find him, and give myself up.
Yes, up, out of this ditch of despair. No one
Need think of me again. I hardly remember
What I was like before to-day, but I think
I was an ordinary woman. No one
Else will remember. 'She was always demented!'
It isn't true: never; until to-day
Struck me like a tornado, God knows from where.
But now I shall give myself up. Do I look
Plain and frightful? It could scarcely matter
Less. But, please God, help me avoid the Duke,
Wherever he may be.

Enter the DUKE, *carrying things salvaged from the fire and over his*
shoulders a string of Chinese lanterns.

DUKE.   He's down at the Temple,
I think, putting up some lanterns which he found
In a box. You'll find him there, presumably
Intent on some small ceremony of his own,
Though fairly uncertain whether it's obsequies
Or jubilation; he's in two hearts about it,

And both weigh heavier than the one he had.
God bless you, Rosabel; hold these; for a time
We thought we had lost you.

ROSABEL.   Did you think so? Lost me?

DOMINIC. You must tell him now. It will be much easier now;
No postponing.   [*Exit* DOMINIC.

DUKE.   It's important that we should offset the smacking of the
     furies
With a little decorous gaiety, with a show
Of holier, if also homelier, flames.
The lanterns, Rosabel. They'll be very pale
Compared with the foment of wild flamboyant rose
We have in the sky to-night; but never mind;
Think what deeds of spring are done
By the glow-worm light of a primrose.

ROSABEL. I started the fire.

DUKE.   How did you come to do that?
A careless flash from your incendiary eyes,
Perhaps.

ROSABEL.   You must believe me. I fired the wing,
To destroy the observatory, to make you human,
To bring you down to be among the rest of us,
To make you understand the savage sorrows
That go on below you. To-day, this awful day,
The violence of a long unhappiness rocked
And fell, and buried me under itself at last.
How vile it was I know. I know for life.
But I didn't know you were there; believe me, I didn't
Know any living soul was there!

DUKE.   O,
O, O, O, Rosabel:

If you had only asked me first.
I could have told you no fire would be enough
To burn down heaven, and while it's there
I shall find some wide-eyed place where I can sit
And scrutinize the inscrutable, amazed
That we can live in such a condition of mystery
And not be exasperated out of our flesh,
As we might be, were it not that flesh
Is interesting, too.
Your fire was too small, Rosabel, though enough
To singe my butler into ecstasy,
And smoke tears into eyes unaccustomed to them,
Mine, I mean. So much I delighted in
Is now all of ash, like a dove's breast feathers
Drifting dismally about the garden.

ROSABEL. Time and I both know how to bring
Good things to a bad end, all
In the course of love. No wonder
'God be with you' has become 'Good-bye',
And every day that wishes our welfare says
Farewell. To-night will go past, as a swan
Will pass like a recurring dream
On the light sleep of the lake,
And I shall be smoothed away in the wake of the swan;
But I can never return what I've lost you, or lose
What I gave, though the long steadiness of time
May long to make us well.

DUKE. So much I delighted in is all of ash.

> [ROSABEL, *giving a moan almost too low to hear, goes out.*
> *Her place is taken by* PERPETUA, *but the* DUKE, *now hanging*
> *the lanterns, hasn't seen the change.*

But the lost world of walls and stairs,
Where I could cosset ghosts for their melancholy
Charm, has let the daylight into me
With a straight left of love. So no remorse,
Rosabel. I love my love, and my love loves me.
Everything goes but everything comes.
We fall away into a future, and all
The seven seas, and the milky way
And morning, and evening, and hi-cockalorum are in it.
Nothing is with the past except the past.
So you can make merry with the world, Rosabel.
My grateful thanks.

PERPETUA. I have to make you understand.

DUKE.   I forgive you:
You can mine the lake so that it bursts
In a hundred and one torrential rainbows
Over the roof of the Carpenters' Arms; you can shatter
Conservatories into a deluge of crystal,
And shoot the cowman's nine insufferable
Children: I forgive you in advance.
I've achieved the rare, benevolent place
Where the irk of the lonely human state
Is quite unknown, and the fumbling fury
We call our life—It wasn't Rosabel
Who spoke then. It was surely Perpetua?

PERPETUA. I have to make you understand. You must
Be patient with me.

DUKE.   God so, it's the little firebird.
Are you rested? Lanterns, you see, to light our love.
I thought we could sit by the cinders
And toast our hearts, if Bates, as he was told to,
Brings the champagne.

PERPETUA.   You have to give me
Your best and gentlest attention. Be
At your most understanding. I need it, if I don't
Deserve it from you. To-night, when we seemed
Closely, and only us of all the living
World, attended by a dragon breathing out
Almost certain death——

Enter BATES, *with champagne and glasses in a basket, and carrying
another lantern.*

BATES.   That Captain Reddleman,
As he likes to demean hisself to call hisself—
Now you're not getting yourselves into anuvver
Critical situation? You can scramble down
Off of that one on your own
Virgin initiative; I'm badgered if I'm going
To throw anuvver expensive rescue party.

DUKE. Matches, Perpetua?

PERPETUA.   No.

BATES.   His illuminated
Lordship Reddleman should ought to have
His brain looked into. In and out, in and out,
In and out of the burning building, like
A perishing nigger in and out of a flaming
Woodpile. And what he says about me's
Enough to arrest a cock in the middle of his crow
And bring a blush to his ruddy comb. It isn't
The language I've been brought up to.

DUKE [*lighting the lanterns*].   The first astonishment
Of creation; after that came the frenzy.

PERPETUA.   Let me
Talk to you.

BATES.   Here's his incandescent majesty
Coming now, wiv his head under the table.

Enter REDDLEMAN, *carrying a table on his head.*

What's the matter, mate; lost your tit-fer?

REDDLEMAN. There's no doubt at all Your Grace has noticed
There are some men are born too small in the soul
To do gratifying deeds, and not sprain all decency.
And 'tis the footman Bates
Who's the diminuendo of all small souls.
He's a demi-semi soul, and that's magnanimous.
I have to put on me glasses, and then search
As if 'twas how I was looking for a louse
In Molly O'Magan's obster-eperous hair.
Would it be here you were wanting the table set up,
Your Grace?

DUKE.   Put it where the wind won't blow;
It's blowing cold. And for Christmas' sake
Will you pair of immortals kiss each other
And come off the tiles?

BATES. I'd just like to know who give him permission
To go measuring my soul? I never done.
I've got it nicely laid away: spotless,
Wiv lavender.

REDDLEMAN.   'Twas a mighty night of miracle,
With Cuchulain at me right hand, and Daniel at me left,
And the smallest soul in the world dashes it from me,
And he naked in his shirt.

DUKE.   Ah, miracles, Reddleman,
Miracles; don't trust them. How far
Can a man journey on a miracle? It's better

To bounce your behind on any spavined hack
Than to straddle a flash of lightning.
Straighten your laurel wreaths, the couple of you,
And remember one another in your prayers.
It seems I have something else to listen to.

Enter REEDBECK *and* DOMINIC.

REEDBECK. Ah, here he is. I'm not what you thought me, your
    Grace.
I must tell you plainly I'm not at all what you thought me.

DUKE. No?

REEDBECK. No. If you ask these men to go, your Grace,
    I shall be only too grieved to tell you what I am.

BATES [*to* REDDLEMAN]. Nuffing to stay for, boy. I'll come and
    see you
Popping yourself in and out of the fire again.

REDDLEMAN. Breakfast, your Grace, at what o'clock?

DUKE.   The morning
    Must wait, Reddleman. I have still
    The rest of the night to consider.

                        [*Exeunt* BATES *and* REDDLEMAN.

PERPETUA [*to* REEDBECK].   Darling,
    Not now. Any day or night of the year,
    There's always time, you can go together, and look
    At the pigs or the winter wheat, and talk your two
    Hearts out; but just this night, and for just
    These five minutes of this night, leave me
    To talk to him alone.

REEDBECK.   I've worked myself up,
    I've reached the pitch now; it would never do
    To put it—put it off; walked much too fast,
    Breath very short, and then heart very heavy,

Imagination—disconcerting—too vivid: I see you
Both up there, no amount of stars
Any use, in dreadful danger, and who but me,
I, whichever it is, responsible?

DOMINIC. Please blame me for that. Do allow me
To know which sin belongs to whom. We shall only
Get confused, father, unless you keep strictly
To your own wrong turning.

REEDBECK.   Extremely difficult
To know where to stop, once you begin to believe
You're not all you should be. Let me see,
There was something worse Dominic said
I had to confess to you.

PERPETUA.   He knows, he knows.
So now, you poor worried Poppadillo, half
Awash with sleep, you can go back
To bed at once, or else I think I shall cry.

REEDBECK. But I don't quite know what you know he knows,
And I think I'd better——

DUKE.   Drink, Reedbeck, I think
You'd better drink. We have something to celebrate,
You and I, which lights me more than the most
Tower-toppling blaze that ever lit
A city lane——

PERPETUA.   Oh, do let me speak to you!

REEDBECK. I've reached the pitch. I've worked myself up
To the point of whatever the point was when I first
Came in. But you're quite right, half awash, suddenly
Woken up in alarm——

DOMINIC.   Now, *think* a minute.

DUKE. Master Dominic: pass to your saintly father
  This glass of champagne.

REEDBECK.   Excuse me. But I know
  There's some good reason why I shall have to refuse.
  Now that my attention has been drawn
  To what must be a myopia in my moral vision—
  Must have been suffering from it all my life,
  I suppose: and to-night feels very latter-day;
  Wrath of God: here we are
  Looking such weak vessels and so temporary
  Among the four terrible elements
  (The rain and the firemen's hose remind me of the fourth)—
  What was I going to say? Yes, yes, I think
  It wouldn't be correct to drink with you before
  I give myself up to Sergeant Bullen.

DUKE.   Drink up,
  And keep your sins for some leisurely angel;
  They've nothing to do with me. Dominic,
  If what appear to be discrepancies
  In your father's books afflict you, let me tell you
  Though they seem unusual they're as much in order
  As Sergeant Bullen's collar and tie. There exists
  A document assigning to your father
  All those percentages from rents and sales
  Which you seem to have thought are misbegotten.

DOMINIC. Do you mean you've noticed the discrepancies
  And legalized them?

DUKE.   My dear conscience-nudging,
  Parent-pesting, guilt-corroded child,
  If I may address you with so much affection,
  The arrangement was perfect. It embarrassed
  Neither of us. Take a drink to wash

Your conscience down. And one brimming for you,
A pale representation of my heart,
Perpetua.

PERPETUA.   It's too full, seriously,
Far too full. You've been good to my father.
Please will you put it down? I know my hand
Isn't steady enough to take it.

DUKE.   Then let me sip
Some away from the western rim
And leave the east for you.

REEDBECK.   Made it legal?

DUKE. There now. Shall we drink
To the babe born in the fire, the crowning of souls
In extremity? As long as we live, Perpetua,
We shall be able to tell how, at midnight,
We skated over death's high-lit ebony
And heard the dark ring a change of light,
While everywhere else the clocks
Were sounding the depths of a dark, unhappy end.
And then we shall be able to say
How an autumn duke——

PERPETUA.   —found that fear could seem
Like love to a silly girl, who now knows
It was fear and not love, wishes you to forgive her,
Wishes she could sink away with the night
Where she won't any more trouble you.

DUKE [*after a long pause, raising his glass*]. Then the toast is: Fear.

PERPETUA. I had to tell you.

DUKE.   Do I
Have to drink alone?

PERPETUA. No. No.

[*They all drink in silence.*

DUKE. Do you think I can't forgive you? I forgive
Both of us for being born of the flesh,
Which means I forgive all tossing and turning,
All foundering, all not finding,
All irreconcilability,
All the friction of this great orphanage
Where no one knows his origin and no one
Comes to claim him. I forgive even
The unrevealing revelation of love
That lifts a lid purely
To close it, and leaves us knowing that greater things
Are close, but not to be disclosed
Though we die for them. I forgive
Everything, my most dear Perpetua,
Except that I wasn't born something less ambitious,
Such as a Muscovy duck.

REEDBECK. I couldn't think
Of allowing such generosity. Legalized!
No, your Grace, I simply couldn't accept it.

DUKE. Reedbeck, my God! For how many years have you
Stood here? You must be very old by now.
I remember you well in happier times.

PERPETUA. Poppadillo,
Why do we all have to get between someone else
And the sun? Keep me from doing this again.

REEDBECK. Whatever you say, my dear; though whatever you're
saying
I really don't know. I'd like to help, but you're both
Talking in my sleep, evidently.

Enter EDGAR, JESSIE, *and* HILDA.

EDGAR. That was a hideous mile or two of driving!
We saw the fire on the clouds, and guessed
It could only be here.

HILDA.   I saw it from home, reflected
In my bedroom window. I tried to telephone
But I couldn't get through.

DUKE.   I must ask you, if you will,
To remember we've been appreciating this very
Minor act of God for more than two hours.
The earth has moved on roughly a hundred
And thirty thousand miles since then,
And histories have been much altered.
I hope the dance was a great success.

JESSIE.   Yes, lovely,
But it's doing myself a great kindness to be able
To sit down. Dancing all hours, and a couple of miles
Of apprehension makes All Hallowe'en
Into a marathon if a girl's not quite
As hale and hallow as once she was.
Is everybody safe?

DUKE.   Safe: I'll not say
'As houses', considering what goes on,
But as safe and suffering as health can be.

HILDA. It's a fortunate thing that providence
Was in her friendly mood to-night
And kept you out of Galileo's lap.

DUKE. Not she. She saw two souls there, happily occupied
At the narrow end of the telescope,
Two star-loving minutiae, male and female,
Perpetua and my unoffending self:

And instantly shot out a vituperative
Tongue. And we were rescued by two
Heavenly agents, Bates and Reddleman.

REEDBECK. God bless them; I've never liked either of them,
But God bless them.

HILDA. And keep them in the heavenly business.

JESSIE. I'll kiss them for it presently. They must
Have got a bit above themselves
To rescue you from there.

EDGAR. And so
You meant to meet there, even this afternoon.
And the only comfort I had, all the way home,
Was that Perpetua was safely sleeping
Away in another house.

PERPETUA. We meant to meet there,
And this afternoon we were lying to you,
And never was a lie less happy for everyone.

DUKE. I hear me whistling down the wind.

JESSIE. We wouldn't
Like you to think we're setting up in competition,
But in our own small way we've met
With a catastrophe, too.

HILDA. Both our cars
Swung in at the gates together, and as our attention
Was all on the fire——

JESSIE. Our wings aren't what they were,
As Lucifer said after his long day's fall.

DUKE. What's the matter with the Fates to-day; fidget, fidget;
Why can't they settle down to some useful spinning?
I forgot to ask you, Hilda (Jessie and Lucifer
Remind me), how is Roderic?

HILDA.   Asleep when I left.
Two ribs broken, and a slight concussion,
Nothing worse. But that was enough to show me
How bad it is to see Roderic hurt, but how
Intolerable it would be to see Roderic
Maimed, or dying day by day; and I sat
Beside him and marvelled, and wondered how
So much could lie there in a human shell,
The long succession of life that led to him,
Uninterrupted from the time
Of time's aching infancy;
In the beginning was Roderic; and now
Haunting the same shell, were a childhood
And a manhood, half a hundred years
Of sights and sounds which once echoed and shone
And now may only exist in him. And though
He tries to be a copy of all his kind
How can he be? He is Roderic-phenomenon,
Roderic only, and at present Roderic in pain.
I felt I must tell you so. This afternoon
I made a cockshy of him, but this afternoon
I could no more truly see him than he, poor darling,
Can truly see half that there is to see.
I must get back home. I only wanted to be
Quite certain no one was hurt.

DUKE.   Rosabel
Is hurt.

EDGAR.   But we saw her with Harry Bullen;
She seemed most vigorous, talking his helmet off;
He was mopping his head with a handkerchief.

DUKE.   Rosabel,
Why? With Harry Bullen? Why should she be?

DOMINIC. Because she thought it was necessary
To her peace of mind. She has given herself up.

DUKE. And I give you up! How, by hell's grand canyon,
Do you know she has?

DOMINIC. She was really very unhappy;
I think I helped her to decide.

JESSIE. But why?
Given herself up for lost, or what?

DUKE. You strapping,
Ice-cold, donkey-witted douche of tasteless water!
I could willingly—Dominic, dear boy,
God would tell me He loves you, but then God
Is wonderfully accomplished, and to me
You seem less lovely, and for this good reason:
You think more of the sin than of the sinner.
Poor Rosabel. Where shall we find her?

HILDA. When
We saw them they were standing by the sundial.
What has she done?

DUKE. Loved me beyond her strength.
We go and get her out of the arms of the law,
However attractive Bullen's arms may be.
Dear Rosabel! And after that we must find
Beds for ourselves away from the smell of smouldering
Memory. Bring along some of the lanterns.
Excellent, blessed Rosabel. Ros-a-bel!

[*He goes, calling her.* HILDA *follows him.*

REEDBECK [*to* JESSIE]. Beds, yes, yes, beds, quite important.
There's one at least at my house if you'd care to oblige it,
Care to make use of it. No more sleep for me
To-night; it wouldn't be wise; I've only just

Managed to digest the sleep I've had already.
In something of a fuddle.

JESSIE.   Dear, I'd get
Into anybody's bed to-night, and sleep
Without a murmur, even in the arms of Morpheus
If he'd give up his lute and let me. Where's the step?

> [*She goes out,* REEDBECK *holding a lantern for her, and he
> follows her.*

DOMINIC. A fine rain raining still. Aren't you coming,
Perpetua?

PERPETUA.   I'll stay in the dry and rest.

DOMINIC. I was hoping to talk to you, to tell you, to say
How responsible I feel for all that fear
And danger, I mean yours to-night. I expect
You think I was very much to blame.

PERPETUA.   No,
Dominic.

DOMINIC. They think I'm altogether wrong,
All the time. But I don't know how that can be.
And yet the whole of life is so unconsidering,
Bird, beast, and fish, and everything,
I wonder how the Creator came to be
Mixed up in such company. Do you think I'm wrong?

PERPETUA. No, Dominic.

DOMINIC [*with a sigh*].   Ethics are very difficult.

> [*He goes into the rain, leaving* PERPETUA *and* EDGAR.
> *They sit in silence for a moment.*

EDGAR. Did you forget I was here?

PERPETUA.   I didn't forget.
But I wish I could forget, and I wish you had forgotten,
This afternoon's brazen lying.

EDGAR.   I have forgotten.
Why should we remember this afternoon
When probably no one else does?

PERPETUA.   But am I sure
I want you to forget as incuriously as that?
I want your father not to be hurt by to-night,
I want you not to be hurt by this afternoon,
I want to be free to make my own way,
But I want to be remembered.

EDGAR.   My memory
Is for nothing else. But, as it happens,
I hardly need it. Over and over again
I see you for the first time. I round
Some corner of my senses, and there, as though
The air had formed you out of a sudden thought,
I discover you. Any memory I had
Vanishes, to let you in so unannounced
My whole body stammers with surprise.
I imagine I love you. And I don't think
You can fairly object, when all you have to do
Is walk freely through my thoughts and round
My heart. You needn't even turn your head.

PERPETUA. Don't say this now. I'm still remembering
I can give pain, and that in itself is loss
Of liberty.

EDGAR.   No, I just mentioned it in passing.

PERPETUA. No one is separate from another; how difficult
That is. I move, and the movement goes from life

To life all round me. And yet I have to be
Myself. And what is *my* freedom becomes
Another person's compulsion. What are we to make
Of this dilemma?

EDGAR.   I haven't the sense to ask.
Whatever the human mystery may be
I am it.

PERPETUA. There's comfort in that.

EDGAR.   Tell me:
Do I seem to you to be only a sort
Of postscript to my father?

PERPETUA.   No, Edgar,
Across and across my heart, never at all.

EDGAR. I begin to notice myself, too,
I must say. Here the little parents come.

                Enter the DUKE *and* REEDBECK.

So now the house goes with a dragging wing.
Are your spirits very heavy, father?

DUKE.   They ride;
No, no, they ride well enough.

REEDBECK [*to* PERPETUA].   Isn't it time
My all night wanderer went to bed?

DUKE.   She will stay
For a moment's peaceful conversation.

PERPETUA. I want to know about Rosabel. When Dominic
    said——

DUKE. I'll keep her story for a rainy day.

EDGAR. And for now the rain has blown over. Shall we go
And see how the last of the flames dance down
To sleep among the ruins, Perpetua?

DUKE. Our peaceful conversation, Perpetua.

EDGAR. Perpetua?

PERPETUA. I'll find my way to bed.

EDGAR. I shall take the liberty to light you there.
To-morrow, then, father.

DUKE. To-morrow to you.

PERPETUA. To-morrow to us all, but not too soon.
I need the soft pillows to make my peace
Before I trust myself to another day to-morrow.

> [*Exeunt* EDGAR *and* PERPETUA. REEDBECK *is almost asleep
> in a chair.*

DUKE. Shall I be sorry for myself? In mortality's name
I'll be sorry for myself. Branches and boughs,
Brown hills, the valleys faint with brume,
A burnish on the lake; mile by mile
It's all a unison of ageing,
The landscape's all in tune, in a falling cadence,
All decaying. And nowhere does it have to hear
The quips of spring, or, when so nearing its end,
Have to bear the merry mirth of May.
How fortunate to grow in the crow-footed woods,
Eh, Reedbeck? But I see you're anxious to sleep.

REEDBECK. I? No, no; I'll never go to sleep
Again to-night, much too disturbed.
Don't know what to suggest I make of anything.
I only hope a quiet dignity
Will meet the case. Civilization is simply
(If I had to define it) simply dignity,

Simply simple dignity; but then
Sons and daughters come into it, most lovable,
Most difficult, and unexpected combustion,
And so forth and so forth. Now le Roi Soleil,
How many children did he have? One legitimate,
Several illegitimate . . . le Duc de Maine,
La Duchesse de Chartres. . . .

DUKE.   Shall I be happy for myself?
In the name of existence I'll be happy for myself.
Why, Reedbeck, how marvellous it is to moulder.
Think how you would have felt when you were lying
Grubbing in your mother's womb,
With only a wall to look at,
If you could have seen in your embryonic eye
The realm of bryony, sloes, rose-hips,
And a hedge's ruin, a golden desuetude,
A countryside like a drowned angel
Lying in shallow water, every thorn
Tendering a tear. Think, Reedbeck,
Think of the wonder of such glimmering woe;
How in a field of milk-white haze the lost
Apollo glows and wanders towards noon;
The wind-blown webs are brighter,
The rolling apples warmer than the sun.
Heavens! you would have cried, the womb
Echoing round you: These are the heavens, and I,
Reedbeck, am stillborn. Would you not?

REEDBECK [*waking slightly*]. And la Duchesse de Condé, I think.

DUKE. So with ourselves; imagine: to have the sensation
Of nearness of sight, shortness of breath,
Palpitation, creaking in the joints,
Shootings, stabbings, lynching of the limbs,

A sudden illumination of lumbago.
What a rich world of sensation to achieve,
What infinite variety of being
Is it not?

REEDBECK. Dominic not fond . . .
Perpetua. . . .

DUKE.   Reedbeck, I have to tell you
I mean to marry. I can still remember,
In my ebbing way, how pleasant it is to love;
An ancient love can blow again, like summer
Visiting St. Martin. A breath will do it,
If the breath comes deep, and deep it has come.
You must give me your felicitations. I marry
Rosabel, when Rosabel
(After six months, I understand)
Is disengaged from custody.

                    [*Only deep breathing comes from* REEDBECK.

Thank you, dear fellow. Rosabel
Would thank you, too, if she were here.
She and I, sharing two solitudes,
Will bear our spirits up to where not even
The nightingale can know,
Where the song is quiet, and quiet
Is the song. Tell me, Reedbeck, before
We leave each other in sleep, where would you say
The lonely moment is coaxing us to go?

               [REEDBECK *gives a gentle near-whistling snore.*

Well, yes, yes, quite so, my little one,
It comes to that in the end.

THE CURTAIN FALLS FINALLY

PRINTED LITHOGRAPHICALLY IN GREAT BRITAIN
AT THE UNIVERSITY PRESS, OXFORD
BY VIVIAN RIDLER
PRINTER TO THE UNIVERSITY